I Can Read

I Can **Understand** What Is Read to Me, But How Do I Work Out **These** Words?

IRENE **LE ROUX**

BALBOA. PRESS

A DIVISION OF HAY HOUSE

Balboa Press books may be ordered through booksellers or by contacting:

Balboa Press
A Division of Hay House
1663 Liberty Drive
Bloomington, IN 47403
www.balboapress.com.au
1 (877) 407-4847

Because of the dynamic nature of the Internet, any web addresses or links contained in this book may have changed since publication and may no longer be valid. The views expressed in this work are solely those of the author and do not necessarily reflect the views of the publisher, and the publisher hereby disclaims any responsibility for them.

The author of this book does not dispense medical advice or prescribe the use of any technique as a form of treatment for physical, emotional, or medical problems without the advice of a physician, either directly or indirectly. The intent of the author is only to offer information of a general nature to help you in your quest for emotional and spiritual well-being. In the event you use any of the information in this book for yourself, which is your constitutional right, the author and the publisher assume no responsibility for your actions.

Any people depicted in stock imagery provided by Thinkstock are models, and such images are being used for illustrative purposes only. Certain stock imagery © Thinkstock.

ISBN: 978-1-5043-1141-0 (sc)
ISBN: 978-1-5043-1158-8 (e)

Print information available on the last page.

Balboa Press rev. date: 05/25/2018

Introduction

Why do some children find reading difficult?

Students who have visual or auditory processing, or short-term memory difficulties, find learning to read and write very challenging. Many of these students fail to keep up with other students when learning or to understand lengthy instructions. They often only follow part of a message because they miss what is heard or seen because of their slower processing speed; therefore, the information that is received can be muddled or confusing to them. They then lack understanding of the critical concepts of their learning. These students have the intelligence to learn; however, they require more explicit instructions, with extra time to process what is heard or seen, as compared to the speed of classroom instruction or other learners.

Students have different learning styles; visual, auditory, hands-on or they may need to talk about what they are learning. Some students require instructions to be repeated, rephrased or different explanations may need to be given for them to understand. When they are attempting to work out unknown words while reading, they can often guess words by using pictures clues; using the first letter of a word and the context of the sentence; using the meaning or sentence structure of the text. These are excellent skills, but when words get too hard or too long to work out or decode, students can get discouraged in their effort to make meaning. When specific needs or disabilities are not addressed, students learn how to adapt or cope the best way they can, and some can give up trying.

Learning how to read involves more than just decoding words. Active readers use visual information, meaning or sentence structure clues, and then they analyse and use what has been read to make meaning. They know the relationship between spoken and written language and how the purpose of reading determines how we read and find the information that we need. They assimilate their knowledge and prior experiences with what has been learned to make meaning and gain understanding. Texts empower us; however, not all students enjoy this privilege as they find the process of decoding words demanding; therefore, they require explicit teaching and extra time to learn concepts and skills.

Other factors to consider

Physical

There could be other reasons why a student may find reading hard. Often, we overlook the very basics of hearing and seeing. Some children cannot understand how letters, words or sentences are pronounced because they have hearing difficulties. If a child is experiencing problems learning, especially in literacy or numeracy, their hearing should be checked by a specialist.

There is more to reading than just seeing letters and words. A vital component of learning to read is whether the student can focus, track or see adequately to read words. Students should have their eyesight examined by a Behavioural Optometrist if you suspect any of these symptoms are affecting the child's ability to learn. Behavioural Optometrists are specialists in the intricacies of focusing, tracking and general eyesight. Make sure you ask the Optometrist to check all of these areas. If there are problems, specific exercises for strengthening the eyes or glasses may be prescribed, to assist with learning.

Processing

Students who experience visual processing difficulties, such as those with a Specific Learning Difficulty, like Dyslexia, often reverse words. e.g. was/saw; lift/fill, or they can confuse letters. e.g. b/d; m/n: u/v: p/b. These are only some of the common confusions that students with reading and spelling difficulties experience. Students who have auditory processing or working memory difficulties can sound out a word, letter by letter, as in c-a-t but say tac. Often, these students can only remember one to two instructions at a time, so when they are trying to work out words with three or more letters or syllables, they find it challenging to recall what they have said or heard. With careful, explicit training, students can learn how to blend groups of letters together, then later chunk through longer words, using syllables to work out, multisyllabic words.

Children who have auditory or visual processing difficulties, process what they hear or see at a much slower rate than other children; therefore, we need to give them more time to respond to instructions and questions to cater for their pace of learning, so that they learn at their pace.

Why use this program?

The 'I Can Read' program is for students who benefit from explicit, individualised instruction, which gives them time to learn at their own pace. These exercises use phonemic awareness, phonics and the knowledge of oral language to identify sounds, letter patterns and the rules used to form words. The activities also help students decode written letter patterns back into sounds and recognised as known words. These skills are fundamental to reading. This program has been developed and used with success to help students focus on letters and letter combinations and learn how to blend them to form words to read and to spell. Decoding is only one of the strategies to work out unknown words and can be overused and underused. Some students guess words or spend too much time decoding words; therefore, by the time they have finished reading a text, they have no understanding of what they have read. This process is a blockage that often hinders them from learning how to read.

It is common practice for many children who have visual or auditory processing difficulties and short-term memory problems, to guess words, using pictures and meaning or grammar clues, in their attempt to work out unknown words. Nonsense or pseudowords are used to help counteract guessing. They have no meaning and can be used to indicate or check if the reader can decode words into their phonemes or sounds, to read or to spell a word. As these words are unfamiliar to the student, nonsense words help them to focus on the letters of words, from left to right, blending and chunking, to decode words.

Reading and writing enjoyment is often hindered because students find it challenging to learn letter sounds and their combinations to read and to write. Make cards for each phoneme and revise them frequently if students struggle to learn in this area. All phonemes are listed in the Appendix. Knowing how phonemes are used to form words enables children to learn how to read and spell. When students have success at decoding words, they are then able to establish the love of reading and gain the knowledge and enjoyment that many of the school population experience. As a teacher and Learning Support Teacher for over forty years, I have found that up to 20% of some school populations may require this one-on-one, explicit teaching.

How is the program organised?

'I Can Read' is a one-on-one program, with tutor and student. The tutor's instructions at the top of each page provide the explanations and guidelines on how to complete the exercises and activities immediately below. Tutors information should always be read first and then instruct the student on how to achieve their section.

The phonemes and skills are systematically introduced, with lots of practice to consolidate learning, using repetition to promote and ensure success for the learner. Once students have the skills of how to work out unknown words like blending, syllable division and using the context and grammar of a sentence, they should be able to work out most unfamiliar words.

Nonsense words are used to introduce each phoneme, concept or skill. Real words are then presented, followed by sentences to help reinforce and use the same phoneme, concept or skill. Nonsense words are no longer used after suffix ending, (ed). Ensure that words are pronounced correctly. If a word is incorrect in a sentence, ask the student if it made sense by asking; Did that make sense? Did that sound right? Do we speak like that? Students should always re-read sentences that are incorrect.

Core sight words are included to learn with automaticity, i.e. no sounding out, to read and spell. Writing sounds and spelling words will reinforce and enhance the learning of the sight words; therefore, spelling is an essential component of the program.

Depending on the student's ability, confidence and stress levels, tutors should judge whether to take the student through one, two or all of the columns or to read only some or all of the sentences of a page in one session. It would be preferable to complete one to three pages of the same phoneme or concept in one sitting.

When a student receives 5 to 10 words wrong on a page, it would be beneficial for them to repeat that page until most are correct. If the student takes more than three sessions on one page, return to revise the specific words or sentences in the next lesson, before starting a new page. When the problem is a real word, not a nonsense word, put that word onto a card and revise it each day until the student gets it correct for three consecutive days. It could also be added to weekly spelling lists to practise the word for homework. Students learn by repetition; therefore, this is a way of reinforcing and assisting with learning.

Tutors should verbally model how to blend letters or how to chunk words into syllables. If a child has difficulties with any concept, you can also say the words with them until they are confident enough to try by themselves, especially at the beginning of the program or on the first day when introducing a new phoneme, concept or skill.

Because students are challenged when processing letters, words or sentences, they can tire quickly. Tutors must continually monitor the student's stress levels. A child's ability to absorb information decreases as stress levels increase. Every child is different; therefore, organise the program to suit the needs of each child. Ensure that a child does not stress or tire, as this is not helpful to learning and it will undermine the confidence that you are endeavouring to develop.

How often should the exercises be taken?

Greater success occurs when the program is taken daily, Monday to Friday. Consecutive days are preferable; however, progress has been achieved with once a week lessons also. Very few students ever complain about doing the exercises because they experience success using this program. Praise all efforts and look for ways to encourage, e.g. getting fewer words incorrect each time.

When this program is used five to ten minutes before a reading session, the student is more likely to apply what they have been learning when reading or they can be reminded of the strategies as they read.

Who can tutor?

Anyone can be a tutor by following the tutor's explanations and directives at the tops of each page. These will help the tutor to instruct the student. Teachers, as well as Teacher-Aides, parents, grandparents or volunteers, can use this program. Refer to the Appendix for helpful tips.

Where to start?

Some students will progress more quickly than others depending on their specific learning difficulty. Tutors must always check if the student knows the sound of all of the single phonemes first. All unknown letters should be learnt before progressing with the other exercises. Once you have established that this is not the problem, then go through one column of each page to determine where the difficulty lies. Often, the third column has harder words. Once the student has experienced more problems on a page, continue from this point, page by page.

How do I record progress?

Place a dot above letters or words that the student found difficult or got wrong. When the word is correct, tick it to show that they have mastered that word. Dating a page can help you keep track of the pace of progress. For tutors to analyse errors, note the date, page number, and column where an error occurs. You may see patterns happening and these issues can be addressed by doing extra coaching in the problem area.

e.g.	Date	Page	column (1, 2 or 3) or sentence number.		
	4/5	P.6.	1. <u>wet</u>	2. <u>left</u>	3. <u>dab</u>
			went	felt	bad

For example, no. 1, the student is not looking at all the letters of the word.
For example, no. 2, the student is reversing letters in words.
For example, no. 3, the student is reversing and confusing the letters b/d. In this case, you need to go to the page that deals with b/d confusion and revise the exercises. Teach one letter at a time, e.g. the (b).

Core Sight Words to Read and Write

Core sight words are the most commonly used words to read and spell. They must be recognised automatically without sounding out, as many do not follow any rule or pattern, for example, *enough, many* and *could*. Words that are not identified automatically to read should be put onto flash cards and repeated until they are known immediately, without sounding out, for three consecutive days. Core sight words are no longer used after Long and Short Vowel Revision.

Core spelling words are the most commonly used words when writing texts. Some words follow no pattern or rule and are tricky to spell. Repetition is an excellent way of learning; therefore, write the words several times, using: say the word, spell out each letter, cover the word and write it and then check. Mnemonics can also help students to remember how to spell any difficult words. Refer to the Appendix or the real word pages at the beginning of the program for examples; however, students can make up their mnemonics for any of these troublesome words.

Writing the sight words assists in the learning of words to read and spelling will reinforce reading. This can be a way of checking if the student knows the words.

Asking questions for sentences and paragraphs

Different questioning techniques help students understand the purpose of reading; to learn the skills and knowledge to become literate individuals. By asking a child questions after they have read a text or sentences, we are instilling the fact that reading is about learning new information and knowledge, not just decoding words. The three levels of questioning that students need to know are literal (factual), conceptual (inferential or clarifying questions) and metacognitive (evaluating or critical thinking) skills.

Ask questions for each sentence if students do not understand what they have read; literal, inferential and metacognitive questions to evaluate or to analyse what they have read. For *literal questions*, ask the student *to retell or remember facts to show their understanding of what they have read.* For *conceptual questions*, ask the student *to apply and analyse what they have read, combining what they know with what the text is about,* e.g. that reminds me of something or someone else, or the word *star* infers that it must be *the night.* For *metacognitive questions*, ask the student *to evaluate,* then *to combine any new information of what they have read, to form a new understanding of that topic.* Ask the student to *critically analyse* what they have read by asking them *if they believe or agree with the view, opinion or interest of the writer.*

What year of schooling can a student start using these exercises?

Any school year level or adult can use 'I Can Read,' if they are experiencing decoding or comprehension difficulties. It is preferable that students know their single phonemes to read and write before they begin this program. Students who take longer to process what they see and hear would benefit from the slower pace of one-on-one tutoring, evident with students who have auditory or visual processing and short-term memory difficulties, e.g. Dyslexia. These exercises can be used from the beginning of the second year of schooling; however, students may need to work through the pages with more repetition of the activities. Adults can use these exercises to improve their decoding and comprehension skills and to learn rules of the English language. These exercises are also suitable for students who have English as their second language.

Praise and encouragement

Remember to praise every effort of the student. Readers are more likely to take risks in a supportive environment where their efforts are valued and accepted. Always model the correct response if the student is having difficulties understanding a concept when learning a skill. Never show your frustration with anyone who is struggling to learn. Be excited when they have success and look for the little improvements, like getting fewer words wrong each day. Provide positive feedback so that the student can begin to monitor and regulate their reading and learning. Students need a purpose for learning to read and write. Encourage them to set goals so that they can have a future full of hope and dreams.

We aim to make students independent and confident learners so that they can enjoy the pleasure of gaining knowledge from reading and writing, to become literate and successful individuals.

Reading and writing empower lives!

Contents

Phonemes and Digraphs

Tutors

Phonemes. A phoneme is a distinct unit of sound in a language that helps to distinguish one word from another, for example *(p), (a), (t,)* is the word *pat,* not *bat*. For students to have a solid grasp of the English language, it is essential to know the individual phoneme's sound to read and write. Practise these regularly until the phonemes can be recognised automatically, without hesitation. Consider making flash cards for the unknown phonemes, so that the student can revise them each day until they can say and write them automatically.

Digraphs have two letters. Some only make one sound: e.g. *th, ch, sh, wh, ph, ng.* You hear two sounds in: *e.g. gl, tr, sm.*
There are silent letters at the beginning of words: *wr, (r); kn, (n); gn, (n); gh, (g).*
There are silent letters at the middle or at the end of words: *mb, (m); gn, (n); bt, (t); st, (s); mn, (m); ck, (k).*
The *ph* says *f* and can be found at the beginning, middle and end of a word.

Read. The student says the short sound, not the letter name. Read down the columns.

z	f	i	ch	st
o	p	s	sh	sp
q	d	w	wh	ph
h	e	a	ck	kn
k	n	x	ng	wr
m	t	j	br	mb
v	g	u	cl	bt
c	l	r	sm	mn
b	y	th	sw	gh

Spell

Cover the above letters and ask the student to spell each phoneme below **or** on a piece of paper.

Tutors

Words are made up of consonants (C), and vowels (V). Every word must have at least one vowel in it. The vowels are: *a, e, i, o, u* and sometimes *y*. (Y) can say 1. Short (i), as in *cyst*. 2. Long (i), as in *my*. 3. Long (e), as in *mummy*. Vowels can have more than one sound, but most of the time they make short and long sounds. Refer to the Appendix for all the vowel sounds.

Short vowel sounds can be quite confusing for some students, especially those who have Dyslexia tendencies, i.e. those who have auditory or visual processing, or short-term memory difficulties. Some children also confuse vowels when spelling, e.g. *cen* for *can; git* for *get*.

It helps to show students where their lips and tongue should be placed to form the letter sounds.
All other phonemes, or letters, are called consonants. These are: *b, c, d, f, g, h, j, k, l, m, n, p, q, r, s, t, v, w, x, y, z.*

Read

Practise the following vowels as many times as necessary, forwards and backwards. Students should say the short sound of each letter. Check that they know the name of each vowel.

a	u	o	i	e	o	u	e	a	o	e	o	u
i	u	a	e	i	u	a	o	u	u	e	o	a
i	e	a	e	a	u	o	u	e	i	u	a	e
o	a	o	i	u	e	a	i	e	o	a	i	u

Use the below exercises to practise any vowels that have been confused. If there are other confusions, write down the letters that have been confused, as per example, and get the student to repeat them verbally.

a	u	u	a	a	a	u	u	a	u	a	a	u
i	i	e	e	i	e	i	e	e	i	i	i	e
o	o	a	o	a	a	o	a	o	o	o	a	a
a	e	e	a	e	a	a	a	e	e	a	e	a

Spell

Students should write the short vowel sound that has been given by the tutor. For extra practice, or for students who learn kinaesthetically, i.e. a tactile or feeling style, get the student to make the letter with clay or plasticine so that they can feel the letter and see it in a different dimension.

Nonsense Words: Closed Syllables

Tutors

Nonsense words have no meaning and can be used to indicate or check if the reader can decode words into their phonemes or sounds, to read or spell a word. As these words are unfamiliar to the student, nonsense words help them to focus on the letters of words, from left to right, blending and chunking them together, to form a word. Some students guess words, as they use meaning or pictures clues, as a way of working out unknown words. Tell the student that these are nonsense words. On the first day of any exercise, if the child cannot blend the sounds, verbally model how to do this and read with the student. They should chunk or combine the sounds, not say the letter or phoneme separately, e.g. *um* not *u-m*. A closed syllable ends with a consonant. Refer to the Appendix for further explanations.

A double consonant of the same phoneme only says one sound, e.g. (ll), (ss), (ff), and (zz). We say *oll* not *ol-l*. Read these exercises as many times as it takes to master the concept. If the student does not learn this concept after three days, move on to the next task, but frequently revise the problem area.

Read: Closed Syllables

op	osh	um
azz	ezz	oss
ib	ut	ad
eff	og	eth
ab	ech	ix
es	ish	uff
ip	om	ell
al	ed	ep
im	ax	oll
et	ic	ag

Spell

Spell the nonsense words that were harder to master. Use the multisensory method of saying each phoneme aloud as they spell. This helps the learner to hear, see and feel as they write, to assist with learning.

Real Words: Closed and Open Syllables

Tutors

Ensure that the student is blending the letters of a word, not saying each letter separately, e.g. *odd* not *o-dd*. Use phrases like, *Stretch the word*, or *Blend the letters slowly*, to explain how to do this. If the student has difficulty blending the letters, verbally model how to do this. Two consonants together, e.g. (ff), (ll), (ss), (zz), (gg), (ck), make one sound and there is a short vowel sound before them. Sometimes (s) can say the (z) sound as in*: has, was* and *is*.

A closed syllable: Ends with a consonant, VC or CVC, as in *am* and *get*. The vowel is usually a short sound.
An open syllable: Ends with a vowel, CV, as in *no*. The vowel is usually a long sound at the end of a syllable.

The (y) acts as a vowel, as in *by* and *tiny*. Refer to (y) in the Appendix for further explanations and practice. Explain to students that (o) can say 1. Short vowel (o), as in *on*. 2. Long vowel (o), as in *go*. 3. (oo), as in *to*. 4. (u), as in *come*. Refer to the vowel (o) in the Appendix for further explanations and practice.

Read: Closed Syllables

is	up	at	in
odd	egg	if	us
it	an	ox	on
am	ill	add	off
as	of		

Read: Open Syllables

no	so	go	to
do	my	by	he
be	me	we	she

Spell

Spell the words that were harder to master. Use the multisensory method of getting students to sound out each letter as they write, so they see, hear and feel as they spell. Remind the student of the different sounds the vowel can say.

Nonsense Words: Closed Syllables

Tutors

In a closed syllable, the vowel is usually a short vowel sound, i.e. CVC, (consonant, vowel, consonant), pattern. Verbally model how to say the syllable if the student has any difficulties. If they are not able to slowly blend these letters as one word, allow the student to break the word as follows, *f-ex,* saying the first letter and chunk the last two letters but always repeating as one word, *fex*. Practise as many times as necessary.

A short vowel sound usually comes before a double consonant: (ll), (ss), (ff), and (zz), e.g. *beff*, i.e. CVCC.

Read: Closed Syllables

mab	beff	roff
rax	miz	moll
mag	zik	soth
bap	fex	yut
tem	hish	whux
ped	chim	sib
ret	poss	wuzz
quem	jeg	bup
tull	hix	thut
shen	sug	zeb

Spell

Spelling enhances the learning of words and enables the tutor to see if the student has understood the concept. Use the multisensory method of getting students to sound out each letter as they spell which helps the learner to see, hear and feel as they write the word, to enhance learning.

Real Words: Closed Syllables

Read: Closed Syllables

hot	sun	hill
red	mad	shot
peg	than	fog
then	will	sob
mat	sit	rug
shed	whip	but
tan	zip	gun
den	top	with

Core Sight Words

Core words are the most commonly used words to read and spell. The student should recognise them automatically, without sounding them out, as many do not follow any rule or pattern. Make a card for the unknown words and repeat until they can be recognised automatically, without sounding out, for three consecutive lessons. Learn to spell the words by writing them 4-5 times using the look, say, spell, cover, write and check method.

The (a) usually says a short (o) sound after a (w) sound. Refer to all vowel (a) sounds, in the Appendix.

are	have	here
was	has	went
his	this	and

Spell

Look at the word, say the word, then say each letter aloud, cover and write the word, then check.

Adding (s) to Words: Closed Syllables

Tutors

Some students do not see the endings of words. They need to focus from left to right, to look at all letters of words. The following exercises help them to focus on the final (s). Adding (s) can make a plural (more than one) or change the verb (doing word).

Read: Closed Syllables

bag	leg	six
bags	cuts	jabs
win	hops	robs
wins	him	ten
dog	hats	when
dogs	pens	chins
run	caps	box
runs	wax	shops
hen	dots	had
hens	zips	then

Core Sight Words

put	they	you
now	come and comes	one

Spell

Students need to learn to read and spell the core words automatically, without sounding them out. Mnemonic is a method used to help students remember how to spell difficult words. Make up a sentence using the first letters of a word, e.g. **Come On My Elephant**, spells *come*. Learn by repetition, Y-O-U spells *you* and you it must be.

Sentences: Closed and Open Syllables

Tutors

Words that students have been learning to read in the real word section will be practised in sentences. Each sentence is a short statement to help students focus on the letters of a word so that they do not guess. Read as many sentences as you believe the student can do without tiring. Repeat the sentences that had errors in them. Praise all efforts.

Ask questions for each sentence, e.g. No. 3. Where did they put the whip? Also ask students if they know the meaning of some words, e.g. What is an ox, dam or van?

You may also take note of any error by writing what was said on top of the correct word, e.g. <u>then</u>.

they

There could be a pattern of errors, so they need to be analysed to see why there is a mistake. In the next lesson, repeat the sentences that had errors in them.

Explain that (ck) is one sound (k) and it always has a short vowel sound before it, e.g. *track.*

Read:

1. The man was here and he went and sat on the big log by the shed.

2. Here is a red sack that has a mat, rug and pegs in it for you and me.

3. Do not come into the den with that whip. Put it on the peg now.

4. This big ox will kick you in the shins, so come here and sit by me.

5. The thin man will run and jog up to the hut and back to get fit.

6. Can you pick pots that do not have odd lids, for Ben and Pam?

7. The duck had one egg and it was in the mud by the big dam.

8. Jed has a bug on his leg so we will put it back onto the wet mud.

9. The sick duck will peck you if you come into the shed with the vet.

10. They put his sacks by the box and went into the hut with Jed.

11. You can now put the dogs in the shed, as the cat is in the box.

12. Can you pick up one bag then come and put it here by my dish?

13. You can now put the big jet and a red van in the shed for the men.

b/d Confusion

Tutors

Many students confuse or reverse the letter (b) and (d) when reading and writing. Students who have visual processing difficulties, like Dyslexia, have to work extra hard to work out if the letter is a (b) or a (d). They tire more quickly than other students because they have to work harder to process letters or words. As they tire, they make more errors. The following are some ideas on ways we can help students to remember the letter (b). Always learn one letter at a time to prevent any confusion. Learning styles may differ, so choose one of the following methods to suit the child.

Visual and Auditory Learners.

Trace over the letter (b) by saying, "*Down the stick, up the stick and around.*" Some students form the (b) as they do a number 6. Trace over the letter with different colours, (rainbow writing). To put this into their visual memory, the student should then hold up the paper, just above their head in front of them, slightly to the left, so that the eyes are looking up at the letter and say each letter name or sound. They should then put the paper down and write the letter and say its sound or letter name as they write. This method can also be used to help remember how to spell any word. Often, we see some students looking up as if to think. They are retrieving something from their visual memory.

Tactile Learners.

Make a letter (b) with clay or plasticine by rolling a stick and a circle, then put them together. Get the student to trace over the letter with their finger, feeling the movement, *down the stick, up the stick and around.* Then say the (b) sound.

Visual Learners.
The bat comes before the ball. The stick before the ball says (b). Put a picture like this onto a card and tape on the student's desk so that they can refer to this for the correct formation of the (b).

If a student confuses or reverses the (b) or (d), revise these exercises and remind them of one of the above strategies to remember the (b). The letter (p) has also been added to the exercises as sometimes this can be confused with (b). Remember to focus on one sound at a time.

Read: Column 1 followed by Column 2. (Read across)

Column 1								Column 2							
b	b	d	d	b	b	d	dad	p	d	d	b	p	d	b	pod
b	d	d	d	b	b	b	bed	d	d	b	b	p	p	d	dud
d	d	b	d	d	b	b	bad	b	b	d	d	p	d	b	pip
d	b	d	b	b	b	d	bud	b	d	d	d	p	b	d	bop
d	d	b	d	d	d	b	dud	p	p	d	d	b	d	b	pad
b	d	d	b	b	d	b	bid	b	b	d	b	p	d	b	bud
b	d	d	d	b	d	b	did	d	d	b	d	p	p	b	dab

Hearing Initial Consonants in Words

Tutors

Students with auditory processing difficulties find it harder to hear each phoneme in digraphs and trigraphs when they say them as one sound; therefore, when first learning two or three consonant blends, slowly say each sound separately, e.g. *b-l* not *bl*. Often, when students say two or three consonants as one sound, they are not able to hear the second or third consonant and this can affect the student's ability to hear each consonant when spelling words. Please note that: (th), (ch), (sh), (wh), (ck), (ph) and (ng) are sounded as one sound.

Read each word to the student and ask them to name the two or three sounds that the word starts with, e.g. for *black*, they should say the sounds (b-l). Note the errors and use these consonant combinations to make other words that start with the same sounds, if necessary.

Explain that (ch) says 1. (ch), as in *church*. 2. (k), as in words *chlorine* and *Christopher*. 3. (sh), as in *machine*. The (chl) and (chr) say the (k) sound of (ch). The English language does not use (kr), it is always spelt (cr).

Read:

Read the words to the student. The student should say the first two or three sounds of each word, e.g. b-l for black.

black	small	brush
snap	click	spill
crab	stem	dress
sweet	flax	splash
frill	twins	scream
dwarf	grin	spring
plan	slab	squeal
scat	press	strap
queen	skid	shrug
glad	tree	

Spell

Practise the combinations that the student found difficult. Students should sound each letter aloud as they write, using the multisensory method, so that they can hear, see and feel what they are writing.

Reading Initial Consonants in Words

Tutors

Students with auditory processing difficulties often find it harder to hear each phoneme of the two or three initial consonants of words. When said as one sound, this can affect the student's ability to listen to each phoneme when spelling words. It is preferable that the two or three consonants be said, e.g. b-l not (bl), or s-c-r not (scr), and not be blended as one sound. Verbally model how this should sound if there is a difficulty saying the two or three letter phonemes.

Read: Initial Consonants

bl	sl	gr
pr	cr	dw
sc	fr	scr
fl	sk	spr
sw	br	str
sn	tr	squ
dr	gl	spl
cl	sp	shr
pr	tw	thr
pl	sm	

Spell

Spell the initial consonants that were incorrect or all if you want to check for understanding.

Nonsense Words: Initial Consonants, Closed Syllables

Tutors

Explain to students that these are nonsense words. The letters should be slowly blended to make the word. Some students respond to the phrase, *stretch the word*. Verbally model how to do this, if necessary. If some students find this too stressful, allow them to chunk as follows, e.g. *d-r-iss, driss*.

A closed syllable has a consonant at the end of the syllable, CCVC, CCCVC or CCVCC; the vowel is usually a short sound.

Read: Initial Consonants, Closed Syllables

driss	cren	dwin
flim	frod	scrop
blid	skem	spreg
sleff	brop	stram
scazz	tross	squitt
blat	gluff	spluff
snam	spub	scrab
clab	twull	sprozz
sweg	prum	strep
plex	grax	squell

Spell

Spell the problematic nonsense words. Ensure that the student is saying each phoneme aloud as they spell so that they can hear, see and feel the sounds that they are writing.

Real Words: Initial Consonants (1), Closed Syllables

Tutors
The letters of the word should be slowly blended. Some students respond to the phrase, *stretch the word.* Verbally model how to do this, if necessary. If some students find this too stressful, allow them to chunk as follows, e.g. *c-r-oss, cross.*

Read: Initial Consonants, Closed Syllables

prod	blot	flex
sped	stems	scrum
press	stub	scab
trap	slug	claps
swell	slab	cliff
twins	crabs	frogs
twigs	cross	fret
drab	smell	skull
drug	smug	skips
snug	grub	spot

Core Sight Words

after	again	some
your	how	what

Spell

Help students to learn spelling words by giving them clues that can help them recall how to spell a word, e.g. *What – w**hat** hat.* Questions start with (wh). *Your* comes from *you.* Make a sentence to learn *some,* e.g. **S**it **O**n **M**y **E**lephant, spells *some.*

Real Words: Initial Consonants (2), Closed Syllables

Tutors
Ask the student to *stretch the word* by slowly blending the letters to form the word. Verbally model how to do this, if necessary. If some students find this too stressful, allow them to chunk as follows e.g. *b-l-iss, bliss.* Remind them to look at the (s) at the end of some words.

Read: Initial Consonants, Closed Syllables

stops	scat	snap
bliss	slot	plots
pram	press	shrug
swims	claps	thud
drop	fret	scrap
slip	skin	squid
cross	brags	split
smell	grins	sprig
flat	trot	strap
crabs	dwell	scrum

Core Sight Words

said	for	all
does	from	who

Spell

Mnemonics can help students learn how to spell tricky words. Repeat the sentence several times, e.g. *She Ate It Down* spells *said; Don't Over Eat Sausages* spells *does; William Helped Oscar* spells *who.* Students can make up their sentences to remember how to spell difficult words.

Sentences: Initial Consonants, Closed Syllables

Tutors

Note the sentence number and word(s) that were incorrect by putting a dot above the word(s). If there are too many errors, repeat the sentence up to three to four times. Repeat this sentence in the next session. If one word is the problem, put it onto a card and revise it until learnt with automaticity, i.e. no sounding out. Remind the student that they need to blend the letters slowly. Verbally model this, if necessary. If time is an issue or the student tires, only read 4 - 6 sentences in one session.

Ask questions for the sentences to check for meaning, e.g. No. 6. What will the men do when they spot the tram? Also ask the meaning of some words, e.g. What does *spot,* mean? No. 7. Had there been a mess on the bed before? What word tells us yes or no?

Remind the student of the sounds that (u) can make, as in *push.* Refer to the Appendix, for all vowel (u) sounds.

Read

1. How can the twins get the fly into the trap for the big frog?

2. Who said that the smell is from the bad clam in that mud?

3. Fred and Zak will have to push the drums back into the shed again.

4. After you hit that stick again, some of your frogs will hop back to us.

5. Gran said we must come back after you drop off the red plums for us.

6. Some men will run and get all of the bags when they spot the tram.

7. What will we do with all of the mess that we got from your bed, again?

8. You can drop some stuff into the bins for us after you come back to that spot.

9. Who can hop or skip from this stick to the dam and back again?

10. How can the men run again, after they go off the track into the mud?

11. A big slug slid by on some wet flax so they will not swim in the dam.

12. Do some of the big twigs come from the top of this shrub by the shed?

13. Does this trap go from the top of the box to here, so we can get in it?

14. Who can run from this spot, then stop here for six claps, then go again?

15. Can the frogs sit on some of the twigs that are in the drum?

16. We got the red spots on our skin after some drops fell onto us from a jar.

Nonsense Words: Final Consonants, Closed Syllables

Tutors

Verbally model how to blend the letters if the student has difficulty reading a word. Allow the student to chunk the word, e.g. *ch-unk*, if they are not able to slowly combine all the letters of a word. Repeat this exercise, as many times as necessary.

Explain that a closed syllable usually has a short vowel sound before a double consonant.

Read: Final Consonants, Closed Syllables

toct	selm	thend
fict	wilm	thrind
seft	kilp	whenk
moft	rulp	tenk
beld	jelt	chint
telf	bult	mont
vulk	somp	lapt
telk	bamp	sopt
zosk	vesp	pust
visk	quosp	shust

Spell

Spell words that were incorrect. The student should sound out the letters, as they write the word.

Real Words: Final Consonant, Closed Syllables

Tutors

There is usually a short vowel sound before a double, final consonant; however, there are some random words that have silent letters or long vowel sounds, e.g. *calm, palm, psalm, drama, raft, craft, yolk, wild, mild, wind* and *both*.

An (a) usually says the (ar) sound when there is an (s), (f), (th), and (lm/m) after it. Refer to the Appendix for all the sounds for vowel (a).

Read: Final Consonant, Closed Syllables

left	help	last
font	lisp	wept
sect	sent	mask
soft	belts	desks
cold	camps	past
held	must	palm
self	sends	fast
golf	wind	just
milk	thanks	kept
bulk	bank	calm

Core Sight Words

any	many	could
would and should	want	before

Spell

Use sentences to help learn and remember tricky words. **M**onkeys **A**re **N**ot **Y**ellow, spells *many*, and *A*re *N*ot *Y*ellow, spells *any*. For *would, should* and *could*, use the first letter of the word, then *O U Lucky Duck*.

Sentences: Final Consonants, Closed Syllables

Tutors

Repeat a sentence if the student makes an error. Put a dot above an incorrect word and repeat that sentence at the start of the next lesson. Read as many sentences as you feel the student can do in one session without tiring or getting stressed.

Remember to ask questions for sentences, using *where, when, who, what* or *why*, so that students realise we must read for meaning, e.g. No. 2. What is a palm? No. 9. Where did they keep the crab? Also, check for the meaning of words.

Remind students that an (a) says (ar) when there is an (s), (th), (f), or (lm/m) sounds after it, as in *last, bath, after* and *palm*. Explain that (a) says a short vowel (o) sound after a (w) sound, as in *wash*. Refer to the Appendix for the other sounds for the vowel (a).

Read:

1. How many men will we have to get to lift that big desk onto the truck, as it must go to the shop to be sold?

2. We do not want to see the palms of your hands on your desk, as they are black from the mud from the dam.

3. Would any of you like to hold up this mask, so that I can see what it looks like, as it is too big for me to hold?

4. How many of the men want to jump off the log and swim to the bank before it hits into the rocks?

5. We crept past the shed so that we would not get hit by a ball from the golf game before anyone could stop us.

6. Who can come and put some cups into the sink for me before I get someone to wash them?

7. We did not want to get too cold, so we left the bank and swam to the rafts and then sat in the sun to get dry.

8. Some big dogs could not drink their cold milk from the small pots, so they did not have a drink all day.

9. Your last crab to be sold could be kept in a tub in the shed before we send it to the shop.

10. How many tents could be lost or swept away by the strong winds that will hit our camp today?

11. Could any of you help me by going to get the cold milk that I left on my desk, as I want to drink it now?

12. We want to send help to all of the dogs and cats that were left outside, as they are in the cold.

Read: Split Digraphs, VCe

dipe	tude	knafe
quafe	keme	zoze
pume	wime	yine
boke	loze	wrame
tebe	pove	thume
dibe	fape	rete
jave	kipe	phebe
zute	hude	wrome
vome	bape	nebe
meve	quode	knofe

Spell

Spell some of the words that the student had difficulty reading. They should sound out the letters of the word so that the tutor and student can hear and see what sounds they are writing.

Real Words: Split Digraphs, VCe

Tutors

If students cannot master this concept after three attempts, make more words for practice. Some students find the VCe rule challenging to master and may need more repetition to consolidate learning.

Explain that (c) can say (s) when there is an (e), (i) or (y) after it. 1. (ce), as in *cent* or *face*. 2. (ci), as in *city*. 3. (cy), as in *cycle*. 4. (cy), as in *bicycle*. 5. (cy), as in *fancy*. Refer to Soft (c), P. 52, for further explanations.

Read: Split Digraphs, VCe

same	tune	knife
quite	homes	zone
time	wide	wrote
takes	case	writes
tubes	pave	game
line	fine	holes
name	Kale	phone
vote	base	cane
mice	races	face
race	laze	bikes

Core Sight Words

each	which	other
use	these	about

Spell

Spell words with which the student found difficult to say, to practise the VCe rule.

Read

1. Could you use that white knife to cut the cake for Dad, before the phone goes again, as I want to have some now?

2. These are the names of the best, five songs to sing and we can use them to have fun as we play games.

3. There are many pink phones, about the same size as these in the case from your home, and they are not for you.

4. Zane could bust a hole in that black kite if he makes it lift up by those trees again, so he should go away now.

5. The men rode their bikes by the ropes so that they would not fall off the path and get wet again.

6. There was quite a big hole in the top of the box, so they used it to get inside to find a place to hide.

7. Both of your tins have quite a bit of rust on the side of them, right beside the long, white stripe.

8. If you want the prize, each one of us must put a tick in the box to vote for the game that we think is the best.

9. After we cross to the other side of the pond, we must rule lines in the sand, so that we can play a game of handball.

10. If you stab the pages with that big pen, you could make quite a big hole in each page and then we cannot write on them.

11. You must race all the other bikes and get to the line before all the others so that we can win the best prize for your Gran.

12. We should use the red and white roses as gifts or prizes for those other games that we want to play today.

Nonsense Words: Initial Consonants and Split Digraphs, VCe

Tutors

Verbally model how to blend the letters of a word or to chunk the letters of the word, e.g. *b-r-ame* says *brame* and remind the student of the function of the (e) at the end of the word, if necessary. If the student gets more than five words wrong, repeat the page, up to three times. Repetition is a method by which students learn.

Read: Initial Consonants and Split Digraphs, VCe

brame	stobe	scaze
blofe	slexe	pluve
flube	prabe	shride
swefe	clite	threde
droke	frune	scrite
sline	skade	squope
crute	bruke	splate
smese	grife	sprixe
flaze	trome	straze
crite	drobe	clume

Spell

Students should sound out the letters as they write a word, so that they can hear, see and feel the letters that they are writing. Remind the student of the VCe rule that makes the long vowel sound.

Real Words: Initial Consonants and Split Digraphs, VCe

Tutors

Remind the student of the long vowel sound when there is a split digraph, VCe. Verbally model how to blend the letters, if necessary.

Explain that (u) can say the long (oo), as in *prune* and *plume*. Refer to other sounds for the vowel (u), in the Appendix.

Read: Initial Consonants and Split Digraphs, VCe

close	bride	crime
quite	drove	flames
froze	grime	glaze
prizes	planes	blade
slide	skates	stripe
spoke	snake	phrase
shade	broke	scrape
globes	choke	swipes
prune	flute	sprite
space	twine	stroke

Core Sight Words

their	goes	large
right	always	water

Spell

Spell words with which the student had difficulty.

Sentences: Initial Consonants and Split Digraphs, VCe

Tutor

If there is an error in a sentence, repeat that whole sentence the next lesson. Explain that the (g) can say (j) when there is an (e), (i) or (y) after it. 1. (ge), as in *gentle* and *cage*. 2. (gi), as in *giraffe*. 3. (gy), as in *gym* and *energy*. There are exceptions, as there are for many rules, e.g. *girl* and *give*. Refer to Soft (g), P. 56, for further explanations. Read as many sentences as possible before the student tires. Stop when there are lots of errors and re-read these sentences.

Ask literal and conceptual questions for sentences, e.g. No. 2. Who might have been doing the test? Ask inferential or clarifying questions, e.g. No. 5. Why would a snake be by the cage? How many cranes would there be? Ask the student if they know the meaning of words, e.g. No. 8. What do the words *bloke* and *mule* mean? No. 9. What does pure mean?

Read

1. Put the plate of red grapes on the mat, right there by those white roses in the water, so that we can have them for lunch.

2. They always put the date and their name on the top of the page before they wrote a long story for a test.

3. The large flames from the bushfire could rise over the trees by the lake, close to where Bruce lives.

4. The smoke from the flames of the outside stove always went into their homes and made many people choke.

5. We always spoke about the large snake that wanted to get into the white cranes' cage, when we were at school.

6. Jake and Mike's mum could win a prize for their large plane made of sand, as it had shells on the sides.

7. When some people dine out, they like to drink wine or coke before they have their grapes and prunes.

8. We spoke to the bloke who came and rode his mule over the sandy dunes into the water of the lake.

9. The little child will give the cat some pure water to drink and then scrape some bones onto a large plate for it too.

10. You could win a huge prize with lots of games if you vote for the whale that has a cute baby, over there in the water.

11. They should scrape a large hole in that huge tube so that they can make a water slide that goes into the water.

12. The black snake always goes right up to the hole in the shed by the water and slides inside.

Nonsense Words: Long and Short Vowels

Tutors

The VCe pattern usually makes a long vowel sound before a single consonant, when the vowel is at the end of the syllable. A vowel between 2 consonants CVC or before 2-3 consonants, CVCC, usually makes a short vowel sound, when the consonant is at the end of the syllable. These exercises will ensure that the student is looking carefully at each word to recognise and remember these general rules. Repeat the page if there are many errors. If the student gets most of the words correct, go to the next exercise.

Read: Long and Short Vowels

pime	drub	strill
pon	zine	queck
lome	wheme	prat
jegs	plun	crine
plab	hoct	flive
stide	wixe	thrim
uss	shrid	wron
spole	chun	tede
flam	smess	cripe
brux	blide	twun

Spell

Spell words with which the student had difficulty.

Real Words: Long and Short Vowels

Tutors

Remind the student of the VCe pattern that makes a long vowel sound, when the vowel is at the end of a syllable, and the first syllable is accented. A vowel between 2 consonants, CVC or CVCC, makes a short vowel sound when the first syllable is accented, and there is a consonant at the end of the syllable.

Model how to pronounce a word, if necessary. Repeat the page when there are many errors. If the student gets all of the words correct, go to the next page.

Read: Long and Short Vowels

same	drag	strap
pan	size	quote
broke	while	plan
jug	plug	phone
plus	bent	drive
stone	wide	rule
theme	these	huge
spoke	them	quake
flame	sniff	frills
flax	bride	blunt

Core Sight Words

more	people	know
because	another	very

Spell

Mnemonics can help students remember how to spell difficult words. Make your own sentence or use the following: *Big Elephants Can Always Understand Small Elephants,* spells *because.* Other strategies also help, *e.g. Pe-ople* spells *people.*

Read

1. After the smog goes, the mist will be white. It will be cold and everywhere will look damp and wet.

2. People know that they could sell their white grapes and very large, red plums from the same shop that they get water.

3. Stop the flames on that fire, as smoke could choke many people or make them very sick.

4. The men should play on their drums as they ride their bikes because they could win another prize for their club.

5. I know some people who would run and hide when they saw a plane spin and twist at shows.

6. The frog jumped into the pond and broke a very thin twig because it made a huge splash as it went into the water.

7. I know that the black dog will take his bone and put it in a huge hole by the shed so that he can have it later.

8. When more people see the size of many of those huge whales in our waters, they may want to save them.

9. Put the sand from the dunes over by the grass, so that more children can play in the shade of their tents.

10. Those children should not swim in the water where snags on sticks could stick into them.

11. Take the knife away from that little child because I know that the blade on it will cut him.

12. I know that the glass in the frame will smash if you drop another stone down onto it, so do not do it again.

13. The knife was blunt and bent, so we could not cut up the huge pile of flax.

Syllables

Tutors

Some students find acquiring oral and written language skills as well as decoding and encoding words challenging, as they have difficulty with phonological processing. These are common characteristics often associated with poor auditory or visual processing and short-term memory skills. Students only recall one or two instructions at a time or remember one or two sounds (phonemes) at a time. A strategy to help students who have these difficulties is to teach them how to chunk words into syllables so that they can sound out longer multisyllabic words.

The Oxford dictionary defines a syllable as *a unit of pronunciation having one vowel sound, with or without surrounding consonants, forming the whole or a part of a word.* Syllables can be felt by holding the hand under the jaw, to feel it drop at every syllable or by clapping and hearing the beat of the word. Show students how to feel or clap the beat of the syllables in words. These strategies will help them sound through longer multisyllabic words to read, as well as spell longer words.

Once children can hear the beat or feel the syllables in words, teach them the general rules of how to chunk words into their syllables. They should also know the meaning of a vowel (V), and consonant (C), before they attempt this section. Students have already had practice reading smaller words, e.g. *CVC/run; CV/go; CCVC/shut; CCVCV/flame.* Write V or C above words to show students these rules, if necessary.

There are three types of syllables: closed, open and irregular. Divide each according to how they are stressed. In closed syllables, e.g. *CVC/CVC,* as in *win/ter,* the vowel is a short sound when the first syllable is stressed and the consonant is at the end of the syllable. In open syllables, e.g. *CV/CVC,* as in *mu/sic,* the vowel is a long sound when the first syllable is stressed and the vowel is at the end of the syllable. In irregular syllables, e.g. *CVC/VC,* as in *riv/er,* the vowel can be a short sound when the second syllable is stressed.

- The number of syllables should equal the number of vowel sounds in a word
- Remember that (y) is sometimes a vowel sound, (e) or (i), as in *juicy* and *apply*
- Sounds such as, (ay), (ai), (ee), (ea), (ou), (oo), are counted as one vowel sound
- The (e) in VCe, does not count as a vowel, e.g. *time*; therefore, *time* has only one syllable
- Never divide digraphs/trigraphs, e.g. *th, sh, ch, wh, str, thr* or *spl*
- Never divide prefixes, e.g. (dis) or suffixes, e.g.(tion), as in *display* and *addition*

Rule 1. Closed Syllables occur when the first syllable is stressed and the consonant is at the end of the syllable. When two consonants follow a vowel, break the word between the two consonants, e.g. *CVC/CVC, win/ter* and *CVC/CV, hap/py.* There are random words, e.g. *wild* and *both* that have long vowel sounds but usually, two consonants together make the vowel before it, say a short vowel sound.

Rules 2. Open Syllables occur when the first syllable is stressed and the vowel is at the end of the syllable. This vowel says its long sound, e.g. *CV/CVCC,* as in *ma/king* and *CV/CVC,* as in *la/ter.* When one consonant follows a vowel, break the word before the one consonant.

Rule 3. Irregular Syllables occur when the first syllable is unstressed, e.g. *CVC/VCV,* as in *div/ide.* Students should try the short and long vowel sounds to determine which word sounds right.

Rule 4. The Vowel (i) can say a short vowel sound at the end of an open syllable when it is an accented vowel or used as a connective vowel. We still divide the syllable before the single consonant, but the (i) says the short sound, e.g. *in/di/vi/du/al, prim/i/tive* and *in/vis/i/ble.*

Nonsense Words: Rule 1. Closed Syllables

Tutors

When 2 consonants follow a vowel, divide the word between the 2 consonants, e.g. *rib/bot*. Do not split digraphs/ trigraphs, e.g. (sh), (ch), (th), (gn), (spl) or (thr). To help students divide words into syllables, you can draw a light pencil line between the 2 consonants or use your finger to divide the word between the 2 consonants, covering the last syllable, so that the first syllable is seen and said, then remove the finger to say the last syllable, repeating the whole word. Model how to do this first.

Ensure that the student is chunking the word into syllables, not sounding each letter, e.g. *rib/bot, not r-i-b/b-o-t*. Verbally model how to do this if the student gets stressed or tired. Explain that an (a) can say a short (i) sound in (age), as in *passage* and a short (u) sound on the end of a word, as in *zebra*. A *schwa* is a lazy vowel sound. Often the unstressed vowel sound becomes a schwa, as in *passage* and *zebra*. Refer to the Appendix for all of the vowel (a) sounds.

Read: Rule 1. Closed Syllables

ribbot	besson	dinnet
fulter	camber	frimtic
granning	pittent	sectern
prontor	ithper	lizzage
bollet	indet	systet
symtop	pottage	ashtip
proglet	rinnert	splittest
umpect	missert	tripler
zobler	grosset	pinnage
treblem	sulter	pintage

Spell

Get the student to chunk the word into syllables and then write the sounds that they hear in each syllable.

Real Words: Rule 1. Closed Syllables

Tutors

When 2 consonants follow a vowel, divide the word between the 2 consonants, e.g. *rib/bot.* To help students divide words into syllables, draw a light pencil line between the 2 consonants or use your finger to divide the word between the 2 consonants, covering the last syllable, so that the first syllable is seen only and said, then remove the finger to say the last syllable, repeating the whole word. Model how to do this first. Do not split digraphs/trigraphs, e.g. (sh), (ch), (th), (gn), (spl) or (thr). If the student gets all of the words correct on the first reading, go to the next exercise. If there are many errors, repeat this page as many times as necessary, to master the rule.

Explain that (a) can say (ar) when there is an: (s), (th), (f) or (lm/m), after it. If the (ar) sound does not sound right, try the short (a) sound and listen to which word sounds right, as in *plastic*. Refer to Appendix for all of the sounds of the vowel (a).

Read: Rule 1. Closed Syllables

winter	often	follow
under	selfish	plastic
number	passage	shortage
spelling	thunder	dollar
dinner	blessing	helmet
adding	master	impact
zebra	filter	possum
symbol	trumpet	system
extra	market	spinning
lesson	printer	percent

Core sight words

friend	before	beginning

Spell

Get the student to chunk the word into syllables, then write the sounds that they hear in each syllable.

Sentences: Rule 1. Closed Syllables

Tutors

Remind the student of the closed syllable rule. Model how to chunk words into syllables, if the student is not confident.

Ask questions for each sentence, especially inferential or clarifying questions (conceptual), e.g. No. 1. Why would blankets be a blessing? No. 6. Where did they buy their tickets? No. 7. What is an umpire? No. 12. What other animals could escape from a zoo?

Explain that the (t) in (st) and (ft) can be silent as in: *listen, often* and *soften*.

Read

1. Give extra blankets as a blessing to people who live outside because it is beginning to get very cold, as winter is starting.

2. Often, my friend likes to listen to concerts when the army plays some songs on their trumpets.

3. Plastic symbols can be used in lessons to help children who are adding or subtracting numbers.

4. Sometimes hostile or angry people do not listen to the beginning of lessons on how to win games and they can often miss out on winning prizes.

5. The army will play their trumpets and trombones for all of the children as they sing their anthem.

6. Your office should advise you on when you can get concert tickets for your friends before they go into the system to buy.

7. There was a shortage of one player for a soccer game, so the umpire asked if a very fast sprinter, who was there with her friend, would play in a friendly match.

8. Please read the passage about the athletes slowly, as it will include a problem and many tricky words.

9. Those vandals should think twice before they commit selfish acts and kill the little tadpoles that are swimming in the rock pool.

10. At the beginning of the list of things that we have to take camping, we wrote the number of plastic knives that we would need to take away with us.

11. It does not matter if there is a shortage of children to attend our school picnic, as we can get other people from the public to come.

12. The zebra and donkey escaped from the zoo and were in extreme danger as they ran down the road, close to the traffic.

Nonsense Words: Adding Suffixes (er) and (ing)

Tutors

When adding (er) or (ing) to a word that has a short vowel before the last single consonant of the word, double the last letter to make the vowel keep its short sound, e.g. *Slep - slepping or slepper.*

Apply the syllable rule of breaking the word between the 2 consonants, *slep/ping* or *slep/per.* Draw a line between the syllables with a pencil or use a finger to divide the first, from the second syllable.

Explain that the (er) can say a short vowel (u), at the end of a word. An unstressed vowel sound becomes a schwa sound, often referred to as a lazy vowel sound.

Read: Suffixes (er) and (ing)

slepping	tipper	mutting
skutter	prunning	shubbing
vidder	choller	munner
flubbing	gatter	thritting
judder	ketter	zuller
ditting	shommer	clubber
chulling	yutting	brelling
wommer	quinning	jubbing
grunning	blopper	happing
thigger	vetter	goller

Spell

Real words: Adding Suffixes, (er) and (ing)

Tutors

Divide a word into syllables between the 2 consonants. Do not split digraphs/trigraphs: e.g. (sh), (ch), (th), (gn), (spl) or (thr). Encourage the student to divide words into syllables without using their finger or a pencil; however, allow them to use these if they are having difficulty with syllable division.

The suffix (endIng), (er) and (ing), should never be divided. An (er) is often a schwa sound, a short vowel (u), at the end of a word. The (er) and short (u) sound are both acceptable. An (er) in the middle of a word, says (er).

Read

sitter	sitting		better	betting
hotter	hotting		cutter	cutting
runner	running		letter	letting
rubber	rubbing		stopper	stopping
digger	digging		slipper	slipping
hisser	hissing		spotter	spotting
supper	supping		dropper	dropping
spanner	spanning		sniffer	sniffing

Core Sight Words

down	long	were
part	new	find

Spell

Sentences: Adding Suffixes (er) and (ing)

Tutors

Remind the student to break a word between the two consonants. Do not split digraphs/trigraphs: e.g. (sh), (ch), (th), (gn), (spl) or (thr). Allow them to use their finger or a pencil line to divide words into syllables if they are not confident enough to divide without these. If the student tires or there are many errors, do not continue. Repeat the sentences that were wrong.

Ask questions for each sentence, e.g. No. 1. What was stopping the runner from running fast? No. 11. What is the meaning of crane in this sentence?

Read

1. A runner was in last place, as the long grass was stopping him from running fast and winning the race.

2. The spanners and hammers were only part of the things used to put the fittings into the large, new kitchen.

3. Most people find that summer is much better with its hotter days than the long cold days of winter.

4. Many people were very happy to see the digger, which came to stop the mud from slipping down the hill, but they didn't like the mess that it was dropping everywhere.

5. The school children had to write letters home asking for new rubbers and pencils, as there were only six left because lots were missing or lost.

6. The long hissing snake wanted to find the hottest part of the road to have a nap because being cold was stopping it from going faster.

7. The huge diggers were jamming up the traffic as they were going down the road because some were bigger and slower than the cars.

8. Many children were stopping to help me find the lost copper ring that I dropped right beside a long ladder.

9. There was a problem when the children, who were sitting at the dinner table, were dropping glitter all over the butter that we were having for supper.

10. Who can find a picture of a slipper, as we need it as part of the setting for our class play on Monday?

11. The large crane will flutter down from the tree beside the river to have a dinner of little fish and slugs.

12. My friend was beginning to get better at running up and down the steps without stopping so that she could get fit.

Nonsense Words: Rule 2. Open Syllables

Tutors

When the first syllable is stressed and the vowel is at the end of the syllable, it says the long vowel sound, e.g. *CV/CVCC*, as in *ma/king* and cv/cvc, as in *la/ter*. Divide the word before the one consonant.

Allow the student to use a finger or pencil to divide the word into syllables, if they are not confident enough to chunk without an aid. Verbally model how to do this if necessary. Repeat the exercises if there are many errors. If there are no errors, go to the next page.

Read: Rule 2. Open Syllables

fenic	muphis	spapit
bupil	creton	loben
zolite	firon	phorale
cutent	mosen	typost
pravil	depane	tifo
cosin	prilen	cutic
spetan	cocat	shibat
woten	pegan	recone
vorus	tariff	wroken
flutile	iver	straban
jatin	depet	sitan
diter	secal	sening

Spell

Real Words: Rule 2. Open Syllables

Tutors

When the first syllable is stressed and the vowel is at the end of the syllable, it says the long vowel sound, e.g. *CV/CVCC*, as in *ma/king* and cv/cvc, as in *la/ter*. Divide the word before the one consonant. Allow the student to draw a light pencil line before the first consonant or use their finger to cover the last syllable, if they are still not confident at dividing words. Verbally model how to do this, if necessary.

Read: Rule 2. Open Syllables

later	basic	polite
tiny	zero	tiger
oval	stolen	unite
tulip	fever	vital
music	spoken	recent
bacon	pilot	delete
local	virus	total
evil	siren	result
focus	aphid	striking
pupil	idol	human
motel	super	spacing

Core Sight Words

better	once	young
school	children	almost

Spell

Sentences: Rule 2. Open Syllables

Tutors

Remind the student of how to divide open syllables. If they have difficulties chunking words into syllables, allow them to use a pencil or finger.

Ask questions for each sentence, e.g. No. 2. Who waved from the plane? No. 6. Why was the token almost lost?

Read

1. A recent virus at school made many children sick with a fever, so almost all of them were at home.

2. Another plane took off after nine o'clock, so the pilot waved to the young children as they went into their classrooms.

3. I know that almost all of the people enjoyed the recent, local concert because they were clapping for a long time.

4. I know that their food was different to mine because the curry dish was spicy hot and it was hard to digest.

5. Young children know that when there is a fire siren, all of the school must go outside to a safe place at once.

6. I almost lost a tiny plastic token after it fell off the table and onto the path beside a little black kitten.

7. He knows that after adding or subtracting a zero to or from a number, that the total will be the same.

8. Most of the hotels and motels in the large picnic spot were down beside the yellow brick road.

9. Because the cocoa icing was runny on their cake, they almost got the last place for their cooking at school.

10. Once Peter and Steven were inside their hotel, it only took a moment to decide that it would be better to go swimming.

11. Did you notice that Mandy made another lovely mural from the yellow and lilac roses that she got from her local flower garden?

12. Once young children go to big school, almost all of them enjoy it better than Kindy.

Nonsense Words: (y) Says Vowel (e) and (i)

Tutors

A (y) says 1. Its sound at the beginning of words, as in *yellow*. 2. Long vowel (i), as in *my* and *cycle*. 3. Long vowel (e), as in *baby*. 4. Short vowel (i), as in *bicycle*.

If the student says the word *July* with the long (e) sound, ask them if the word sounds right or if it makes sense, then get them to try the long (i) sound. Often, this is referred to as, *flipping to the other sound(s)*.

Explain that often when there is a word starting with the prefix, e.g. *re* or *de*, the ending (y) says a long (i) sound, as in *defy* and *rely*.

Read: (y) Says Vowel (e) and (i)

loby	sanny	strimy
diddy	swy	shry
jutty	quetty	drechy
dy	shiby	phiny
quy	stummy	dely
rinny	zily	spry
smy	hinny	phummy
wommy	chuppy	tryle
printy	dwy	fety
budy	huby	scrimy
mimmy	soply	thry
sply	scry	cryle

Spell

Real Words: (y) Says Vowel (e) and (i)

Tutors

Remind the student that (y) acts as a vowel sometimes. A (y) says 1. Its sound at the beginning of words, as in *yellow*. 2. Long vowel (i), as in *my* and *cycle*. 3. Long vowel (e), as in *baby*. 4. Short vowel (i), as in *bicycle*. If the student says the word *deny,* using the long (e) sound, ask them if it sounds right, then remind them to flip to the long (i) sound.

Remember the open syllable rule breaks words before one consonant and in between two consonants in a closed syllable.

Read: (y) Says Vowel (e) and (i)

lazy	tidy	stripy
baby	daddy	spiky
shiny	spiny	style
lady	reply	softly
tiny	bony	symbol
pony	type	system
rely	Tony	bicycle
duty	fury	baggy
July	deny	funny
crazy	ruby	typing

Core Sight Words

number	follow	sentence
answer	picture	often

Spell

Sentences: (y) Says Vowel (e) and (i)

Tutors

Remind the student of the syllable rule breaks for open and closed syllables. If the student is having difficulties with words, model how to chunk the words into syllables. In the word *answer*, the (w) is silent.

Reduce the number of sentences to read, if there are many errors or if the student tires. Ask questions for sentences, e.g. No.1. Why did they number the sentences? No. 2. What is a paddock? No. 6. What made the sticks slimy? No. 12. What season would it be?

Read

1. Kerry and Trudy want the children to number their sentences, as they had the answers to their request for help.

2. Trudy has a large picture of a black pony that would often follow the baby to the paddock.

3. I know why many silly answers in my sentences were funny and often crazy for some people.

4. Often, a lady on a small bicycle would follow other people because the type of bike she rode was not fast.

5. The stripy zebra was not happy to follow the puppy into the muddy water because it was cold.

6. A large number of spiky sticks were slimy because they were kept in water for over twenty days.

7. Only reply to number five with your answers to why we should try to keep our work tidy because I want to read them.

8. In a funny picture of yummy food, the jelly was ruby red and it was shiny in the middle.

9. The baby will often cry if it is hungry, so please give it a dummy as well as a bunny so it can play.

10. I only want twenty sentences from the class, with the answers to why some boxes were empty and many were broken.

11. It was not very funny when a large python slid between the tall pylons next to my home, last July.

12. Some children were trying to pick the pretty buds off many of the cherry trees down by the shed.

Nonsense Words: Suffix Ending (ed)

Tutors

Add the suffix (ed) to the end of a verb (doing word), to indicate the past tense, i.e. showing that something has happened. Explain these general rules to the student:

1. When a word ends with (t) or (d), as in *wanted* and *added,* the (ed) says, (ed) or (id), depending on peoples' accents.
2. When a word ends with a blowing sound: (k), (s), (f), (x), (p), (ch), (sh) or (th), as in: *thanked, passed, sniffed, boxed, jumped, watched, wished* and *birthed,* the (ed) will say a (t) sound. Spell the (t) sound with an (ed).
3. In other words, the (ed) says (d), as in *loved*.

Often (a) says (ar) when there is an: (s), (th), (f) or (lm/m), after the (a). Refer to the Appendix for all of the vowel (a) sounds.

Read: (ed) can say: (ed/id*)*, (d), (t)

dinked	toved	gatched
silled	idded	hished
thated	pished	jifted
punked	vedded	clasted
shumped	splided	draved
shaled	sunted	nated
tented	blashed	epened
chissed	dommed	bepped
linned	drefted	chiffed
lessed	fanded	trided
taned	damed	jinded

Spell

Real Words: Suffix Ending (ed)

Tutors

1. When a word ends with (t) or (d), as in *wanted* and *added,* the (ed) says, (ed) or (id), depending on peoples' accents.
2. When a word ends with a blowing sound: (k), (s), (f), (x), (p), (ch), (sh) or (th), as in: *thanked, passed, sniffed, boxed, jumped, watched, wished* and *birthed,* the (ed) will say a (t) sound. Spell the (t) sound with an (ed).
3. In other words, the (ed) says (d), as in *loved.*

Often (a) says (ar) when there is an (s), (th), (f) or (lm/m), after the (a). Refer to the Appendix for all of the vowel (a) sounds.

Read: (ed) can say: (ed /id), (d), (t)

looked	loved	matched
called	added	fished
shouted	wished	sifted
thanked	needed	tasted
jumped	cried	saved
stayed	planted	punched
wanted	messed	opened
missed	named	happened
pinned	lifted	hopped
passed	landed	sniffed

Core Sight Words

first	word	around
between	enough	began

Spell

Sentences: Suffix Ending (ed)

Read

1. The runners missed the track that led to the opening of the forest and they ended up on a path that came to a paddock.

2. We lifted up the paper and pinned it to the wall as someone punched a hole in it and messed up our game.

3. My friend cracked open some nuts and then we snacked on some before lunch. We added some to our dinner and began to eat some more, as they tasted so good.

4. Many people clapped and thanked the sick runner as he raced around the track for the last time, after a very long race.

5. The men missed the first bus because they all raced down the road, around a corner and slipped over.

6. Six children picked some apples then walked and sat down under a tree before they began to eat some for lunch.

7. My friend liked playing with Kane because he loved to play with people who enjoyed making up fun games.

8. A player pitched the first ball and the batter missed it, so he ran to first base and then stopped running; therefore, they lost the game.

9. The children checked to see if the webbing between the duck's webbed feet was cracked, as it may have needed to go to the vet to be fixed.

10. Some swimmers slipped into the muddy water and had to be pulled out before they almost went between some rocks.

11. We lifted the rafts into the water then paddled around all of the pylons before we finished paddling for the day.

Real Words: Rule 3. Irregular, Unstressed Syllables

Tutor

An irregular syllable occurs when the first syllable is unstressed and the last is stressed, e.g. CVC/CV, as in *riv/er* and CVC/V, as in *cop/y*. Allow the student to try both vowel sounds, e.g. *ri/ver* or *riv/er*, and listen to which word sounds right. If the student finds this difficult, model how to say both ways and ask them which one makes sense or sounds right.

Read: Rule 3. Irregular, Unstressed Syllables

river	lovely	study
never	credit	venue
using	over	travel
edit	model	lazy
forest	Adam	cabin
ever	divided	volcano
divide	loving	memory
copy	final	family
very	body	planet
even	shadow	melody
cover	gather	comedy

Core Sight Words

every	money	through
walk	together	thought

Spell

Sentences: Rule 3. Irregular, Unstressed Syllables

Tutor

An irregular syllable occurs when the first syllable is unstressed and the last is stressed, e.g. CVC/CV, as in *riv/er* and CVC/V, as in *cop/y*. Remind the student that they need to listen to the words as they read, to hear if they make sense, e.g. *ri/ver* or *riv/er*.

Ask questions for each sentence, e.g. No. 2. What kind of power were they making? No. 4. What do we need to be able to stand and walk? No. 6. Why did the children walk through the forest? No. 11. What is a grader?

Read

1. We walked together through the muddy water of the river before we went between the trees into the huge forest.

2. We cannot make enough money from power when the sun cannot shine through smoke or if there is a shadow on our shed from a large volcano.

3. People should never travel through a forest and stop to make a fire because if embers are left, they could start a huge bushfire.

4. The students will study a model of the body to see how the bones of the spine together help the body to stand so we can walk.

5. Our family thought that we would all walk to the venue for the comedy concert, as we wanted to sing melodies from the show together.

6. Some children walked through a forest to get a video of some people who were driving big trucks too fast and prove that they should be punished.

7. We thought that we had collected enough money from our school walkathon to help to pay for doctors to study why almost every student got sick last winter.

8. A lovely lady covered the model of my planet that had dry rivers and a volcano on it so that it didn't get wet from splashes of water.

9. We thought that there was enough money to buy roses to cover the huge dining room table at the venue, plus give some to every person.

10. Adam told everyone never to swim through the swift water between rocks, even in a shallow river, just to be together and have fun with friends.

11. We thought the cabin in the forest was almost knocked down by a grader that was travelling too fast around the final corner.

Real Words: Long and Short Vowel Revision

Read: Open and Closed Syllables and VCe

tap	hop	slides
hide	hiding	tapping
hope	hopped	cute
din	dining	hoped
taping	tape	hidden
hopping	hides	taped
dine	hid	dinner
tapped	pinned	ridden
riding	pipped	rubber
hugest	slim	drop
piping	glitter	grades

Core Sight Words

whose	won't	don't
what's	couldn't	should've

Spell

Sentences: Long and Short Vowel Revision

Tutors

Remind the student of the rules for making long and short vowel sounds and the syllable divisions.

Ask questions, e.g. No. 4. Why would the pony need more food? No. 5. What was hiding in the rubbish bin? No. 8. What is a traffic jam?

Read

1. We don't want to hide that funny little frog that is hopping beside the river, on the green grass, in the shade of the tent.

2. The tiny ship couldn't glide through the slimy water in the river, so it stopped beside the bank.

3. They won't be riding that tractor through the muddy water in the river, as it doesn't have large tyres.

4. What's going to happen to Max, the pony, if he doesn't have enough food? We are hoping that someone will find him some more in a moment.

5. We couldn't find the final copy of the notice, as we didn't see it hiding under the folder in the rubbish bin.

6. When petrol costs too much and we don't want to use a car, people could ride their bikes to get to places.

7. We should've gone shopping instead of going out for dinner when we found out that dining out would cost us too much.

8. We couldn't go directly to Jake's home as there was a delay on the road because of a blockage from a huge traffic jam.

9. We were waving at the person whose pony almost knocked me over this morning.

10. People were hoping that the writers were planning to publish a book in memory of their family.

11. We don't know whose spade was used to dig up the plants in the native garden at the school.

12. That student doesn't have time to tune his guitar before his music concert begins.

Real Words: (ee) and (ea) Sounds

Read: (ee) and (ea) Sounds

head	great	break
keep	seen	repeat
bread	please	beetle
free	steam	teacher
read	easy	reader
meat	heavy	instead
leaf	tease	breath
been	meant	leader
ready	cheese	season
team	steak	breakfast
each	wheat	degree
neat	clean	peach

Spell

Sentences: (ee) and (ea) Sounds

Read

1. Please divide the right-hand side into heavy items and the left-hand into tiny objects and then add the total to find out how many we have.

2. The teacher read a lovely story about how an eagle was meant to weave a golden leaf into its nest.

3. The teacher agreed that when wheat and cheese are green, we should not eat them, as they can affect our health and could make us very sick.

4. Instead of breakfast at home, we dined out at a huge cabin in the forest and then, later on, went down the street for coffee.

5. The stronger team hoped that it would be easy to win the game, but they got beaten by a weaker team.

6. The peach tree made a shadow over the dining room table in the morning, but it didn't spread onto the floor until later in the day.

7. Lots of tiny beetles landed on the bread and cheese, so people didn't want to eat any; therefore, we needed to buy more.

8. You did agree that it wouldn't be safe to put a heap of sand on the steep path; therefore, could you please clean it off?

9. Everyone wanted the green toffees; however, some mean people tried to hide them, as they tasted so good.

10. The sick person hoped that their health would get better, so they decided to eat only lean meat and leafy green plants.

11. As the person spoke, the steam from his breath showed us that the weather was freezing outside.

Real Words: (ay) and (ai) Sounds

Tutors

An (ay) says 1. Long vowel (a) sound, as in *day*. 2. The (ay), as in *says,* can either say the long vowel (a) or a *schwa,* short (e), depending on the accent of a person.

Usually, the letters (l), (n), (r) and a few with (t), (d), and (m), follow (ai). Any other letter is uncommon. An (ai) says 1. A long vowel (a), as in *train*. 2. The short vowel (i), as in *certain,* when the (ai) is in the second or third syllable.

Often, when two vowels are together, the second vowel is silent or vice versa. If the word does not sound right, try both sounds and listen and decide which word sounds right, e.g. as in *maintain.* Remind the student of the syllable division rules. Never divide a prefix or suffix.

Read: (ay) and (ai) Sounds

played	claim	sprayed
again	contain	maintain
always	dismay	waiter
mail	curtain	mountain
crayon	bargain	fountain
afraid	sailor	brain
painting	chain	nailed
array	display	remain
spray	essay	yesterday
certain	captain	villain
pain	strain	relay

Spell

Tutors

Assist the student, by showing them how to chunk words into syllables, if needed. Remind them to listen for meaning as they read and to re-read the sentence if it doesn't make sense.

Ask questions for the sentences, e.g. No. 2. Why might the waiter have to repeat the order? No. 6. What is a referee?

Read

1. One day when we were on holiday in the Cayman Islands, we remained by a fountain for a long time to get sprayed because it was a very hot day.

2. Today the waiter had to repeat the order of coffee and teas because the sailors were from Spain and Egypt.

3. Yesterday, I looked in the mail for a booklet that contained a featured holiday in New Zealand.

4. There was a great array of sprays on display for Mother's Day and you could always get a bargain price for them late in the day.

5. During this season the hail and rain will certainly delay the painting of the fountain in the middle of the shopping centre.

6. The captain tried to bargain with his team because they were getting beaten, but the referee told him to be quiet.

7. Yesterday, some children wrote an essay about villains and displayed a photo of them, so everyone was certain to read their story.

8. The sails made a shadow over the creek so that the baby quails could drink water and stay out of the heat.

9. Some people wanted to paint the old train which was on display at the top of a steep mountain, railroad track.

10. The snail bait was laid because it was going to rain and we didn't want our daisies to be eaten.

11. Runners in a relay could sprain an ankle if they speed up and jump over a drain too fast.

12. Yesterday, we saw a display that contained many paintings of mountains in Spain.

Real words: Soft (c): (ce), (ci), (cy)

Tutors

A (c), followed by an (e), (i) or (y), usually says (s), as in *cent, city* and *cycle*. This rule is the soft (c) rule. 1. The (ce) and (cy) says (s) and come at the beginning, middle or the end of a word. 2. The (ci), says (si), as in *city*. 3. The (ci) says (sh), as in *special*.

Verbally model how to divide words into syllables, if the student has any difficulties and help them to pronounce words correctly.

Read: Soft (c): (ce), (ci), (cy) Sounds

nice	price	success
race	device	cyclone
city	acid	placid
dance	pencil	concern
face	Greece	civil
mice	fence	centre
advice	grace	France
police	cinema	excite
racing	force	central
cycle	decimal	cellar
fancy	cell	cymbal
decide	celery	entice

Spell

Tutors

When a (c) is followed by an (e), (i) or (y), it usually says (s), as in *cent, city* and *cycle*. Students should be monitoring what they read and listen to words in the context of the sentence to determine which phoneme sounds right and re-read the sentence if it doesn't make sense.

Ask questions, e.g. No. 2. Why would the mice make their nests by the celery patch? No. 6. What does placid mean?

Read

1. Many people called the police for help after the cyclone finished because their homes were broken and they thought that many other homes in the city would also be.

2. The mice made their homes between the dark cellar walls of the garden shed, that was beside the celery patch.

3. The success of the dancing at the circus excited and enticed many children to attend a great many more shows.

4. The student who came to dance classes every day was pleased to accept a prize for his efforts and success.

5. The children recited their French poems at a concert which was held in a cinema in the middle of the city, Nice, which is in France.

6. The lovely kind faces of the teachers showed us that they were placid and showed mercy and grace to everyone.

7. "You must know where to put the decimal between the numbers when you put the price on that bicycle," explained the teacher.

8. Could you please race your bicycle to the place between the broken fence and the centre of the playground?

9. The cakes were just one of the nice foods that enticed friends to come to her party at the central cinema, on the second of December.

10. The people did not accept the advice of the police; therefore, cars were racing through the city centre today.

11. In some cities in Greece and France, you can go to see all of the different fancy dresses that they dress up in, to do their formal dances.

Tutors

There are four sounds that (oo) can make. The first two are the most common. 1. The short sound, as in *look*. 2. The long sound, as in *food*. 3. Short vowel (u), as in *flood* and *blood*. 4. (or), as in *door, poor, floor* and *moor*. Try the different sounds and listen to which word sounds right and flip the sound until the word sounds right.

Read: (oo) Sounds

good	shook	blooming
door	broom	poor
wood	looked	sooty
look	groom	booklet
foot	blood	footpath
roof	proof	foolish
book	floor	cooking
room	food	booked
stood	shoot	flood
root	boot	classroom
mood	wool	moor
took	pool	woollen

Spell

Tutors

Remind the student of the sounds that (oo) can make. They should listen to the words in the context of the sentence to determine which sound sounds right and re-read the sentence if it does not make sense.

Ask questions for sentences, e.g. No. 1. Why didn't the goose have enough food? No. 10. What mood would they have shown and why?

Read

1. How could that poor old goose with white feathers have enough food to eat if the mice took most of it?

2. They filled the pool with too much water and it almost flooded the path by the classroom.

3. The blood on her foot was proof that she made the mess on the floor of the playroom.

4. We took a broom to sweep up the black soot that was over the footpath next to our classroom.

5. We chopped enough wood for the fire because it would be foolish to have nothing to cook our food on at our camp.

6. The boom from the shooting of the canon gave the moose such a shock that it shook water all over the floor of its cave.

7. Who stood on the cheese, then wiped it all over the door of the cooking shed that is down by the pool?

8. A brook is a river that runs through paddocks in the English moors and they can get flooded when it rains too much.

9. He took the broom and swept the floor because soot came down the chimney into the dining room.

10. We looked at their faces and saw what mood they were in, as they stood by the broken footpath.

11. We looked at a booklet to see if we could buy good food for our hungry chooks so that they could lay enough eggs for our breakfast.

12. We took a silver spoon to give food to the bride and groom at their wedding, at noon.

Read: Soft (g): (ge), (gi), (gy), (dge), (age) Sounds

orange	giraffe	message
gentle	gym	longer
large	village	pledge
bridge	fridge	gymnast
huge	logic	stage
rage	manage	judge
lodge	tragic	bandage
hedge	digger	energy
age	general	manager
ginger	postage	tiger
edge	damage	cabbage
caged	Germany	digit
giant	girl	sausage

Spell

Sentences: Soft (g): (ge), (gi), (gy), (dge) and (age) Sounds

Read

1. The large, ginger cat that was found under the bridge was given to Gemma who fed and looked after it.

2. The huge, orange and cream truck broke the hedge and damaged the edge of its large trailer when it crashed.

3. A strange animal liked to swim at the beach and managed to dodge the rocks of the long, spiky reef.

4. Be gentle with that white goose in the box, as the giant tiger almost ate it for dinner yesterday.

5. People are sure to judge the driver of a truck who had a tragic accident beside the bridge that went over a windy river.

6. The captain of the team put her badge on the edge of her jacket pocket before she quickly walked off the stage.

7. The beaver had a lodge in the middle of the stream; therefore, it managed to escape from all of the strange beasts that wanted to eat it.

8. The giraffe damaged the huge, high display at a venue in the game park, so the village had to be closed.

9. Beat the fudge, then put it in the fridge to cool down, before Mrs Rogers and her friends eat it.

10. People lodged their complaints against the changes that allowed having more caged animals live in cities.

11. The children didn't eat their porridge and bread; therefore, they may not have enough energy to go and play.

Real Words: (ow) Sounds

Tutors

When a vowel follows the letter (W), the vowel changes its usual sound. This is a (W) controlled vowel.

The (ow) phoneme can say 1. Long (o) sound, as in *slow*. 2. (ou), as in *how*. The long (o) sound is usually used at the end of a word and the (ou) sound, in the middle of a word.

Remind the student to listen to the word and if it does not sound right, try the other sound. Verbally model how to pronounce a word and how to break the word into syllables, if necessary.

Read: (ow) Sounds

down	brow	narrow
owl	grow	crowded
bow	howl	frown
slow	shower	following
know	tow	sparrow
brown	town	known
blow	yellow	owner
below	window	tomorrow
power	clown	rowdy
grown	show	towel
flower	glow	allowed
powder	pillow	rowed
crowds	follow	slowest

Spell

Tutors

Remind the student to re-read a sentence if it does not make sense. If one sound does not sound right, try the other. Some tutors use the term *flip* to the other sound, e.g. *shou or show?*

Ask questions for sentences, e.g. No. 7. Why would the birds fly away? Ask for the meaning of some words, e.g. No. 8. What is a yellow creeper?

Read

1. The owner of a yellow flag waved it from the window to show the crowd where he was.

2. He felt drowsy, so he had a quick shower, fetched his pillow and yellow blanket and then lay down to sleep.

3. Tomorrow, the general public will have to clean up the city shops, as the snow had blown through most of the open windows.

4. We followed the owner of a brown car to tell them that they had left a yellow towel and a gown lying on the boot.

5. At gymnastic practice, the judge showed the gymnasts how to flip slowly on a long, narrow beam.

6. The powerful winds of the cyclone had blown out windows and knocked down a display in the playroom.

7. The mower went between the grape vines and chased away the owl and crows that were sleeping in the trees.

8. The petals of the yellow creeper that had grown on the fence had been blown away by the powerful wind.

9. The rowdy crowd kept us awake; therefore, we were so drowsy that we wanted our pillows so that we could have a snooze in the afternoon.

10. The clown stood behind the crowd and showed everyone the magic trick. There was a narrow trap door in the wall.

11. A sparrow made its nest on a narrow window ledge beside a flower box, just under the power lines.

Real Words: (ew) Sounds

Tutors
A (W) controls vowel sounds, by changing its usual vowel sound to make a new sound, so (ew), says 1. Long (u), as in *new*. 2. Long (oo), as in *blew*. 3. Long (o), as in *sew* and *sewn*. Other words with (ow) have been added to the list, to ensure that the student is looking carefully at all of the letters of a word and not just guessing.

Read: (ew) Sounds

new	knew	nephew
few	power	tomorrow
sew	threw	newt
grew	jewel	window
town	drew	sinew
sewn	blew	mildew
news	stew	flower
dew	below	pewter
ewe	chew	rowdy
snow	flew	screw
slow	flow	known
renew	jeweller	crew
yew	screwed	renewed

Spell

Tutors

Remind the student of the sounds that (ew) can make. Encourage the student to skip an unknown word and read on to the end of the sentence, then re-read the sentence using the meaning or context of the sentence, to work out the unknown word. If they still do not know the word, help them to sound it out.

Ask questions for sentences, e.g. No. 6. Where were the flowers? No. 7. What caused the damage to the trees? No. 9. Who are the crew of a plane?

Read

1. The crew flew the plane over the bottom of Africa before landing in the city of Cape Town, which is in South Africa.

2. Andrew withdrew from his attempt to swim in the next Olympic Games because of injury, so he flew back home with his friend Lewis.

3. Stewart had to decide whether he would eat more of his steak because it had too much sinew in it and it was hard to chew.

4. At seven o'clock in the morning, the dewdrops on the trees looked like jewels, as the sun was shining on them.

5. Lewis grew a yew tree which had strange blossoms, with fewer flowers on the inside branches of the tree than on the outside.

6. Mr Brown drew a picture of yellow roses in a pewter vase that was standing near a bowl on the edge of a jeweller's bench.

7. In the evening news, we saw that the cyclone blew over many giant trees and damaged lots of homes in Drew and Gemma's hometown.

8. My nephew grew ginger so that he could make a brew of ginger beer and use some to add to his stew that he was cooking for dinner.

9. Mr Newton, the pilot, and the crew of his plane ate stew and a few other meals as they flew overseas.

10. We knew we had to fix the barge with a few screws and some nails so that it was safe to take the cars across the wide river.

11. Lewis stewed lots of yummy apples to make a pudding for our lunch and then he made a brew of tea for us to drink.

12. The carpenter had to renew some of the rotten planks on the deck; therefore, he had to take them off and then screw on new ones.

Real Words: (wa), (qua), (squa), Sounds

Tutors

When there is an (a) after a (W) sound, it says 1. Short vowel (o), as in *was*, *quad* and *squad*, as the (qu), says (kw). These are (W) controlled vowels. 2. Long vowel (a), as in *wake*. 3. Short *vowel* (a), as in *wax* and *wag*. Remind the student to *flip* or use all of these sounds, until the word sounds right.

Read: (wa), (qua), (squa) Sounds

was	squash	waiter
want	wake	wallaby
what	squatter	squalor
wash	quarrel	warrior
quad	wander	wallet
squad	waltz	wallop
swat	swamp	Warren
wand	whatever	quality
wax	wasp	Wanda
swan	wade	wattle
squats	wagged	swallow
watch	squalid	walrus
waddle	waffle	squabble

Spell

Tutors

Remind the student that the (W) controls the sound of the (a). There are some exceptions, so the student should try the other sounds for (wa) and listen to which word makes sense in the context of the sentence.

Ask questions for the sentences, e.g. No. 2. How could they use the money? No. 9. What does shrink mean? No.11. What are the two meanings of swallow?

Read

1. The black swan waddled over to the edge of the water beside the swamp and washed her feathers.

2. After we visited the slums and witnessed the squalor that the squatters lived in, we hoped people would open their wallets and give money to help them.

3. Please swap that watch and wallet for a copper or gold chain, so that you don't waste any more of our time.

4. The wallaby jumped over the large wattle bush and squashed a wasp which had tried to sting him on his long tail.

5. The huge walrus wandered over the road and began to swallow all of the food that Warren and Wanda had given it.

6. Wanda ate her waffle then wandered outside to watch Warren wash and wax his new wagon.

7. I tried to wallop the wasp that tried to sting me as it flew out of the yellow wattle flowers.

8. Warren and Wanda had a squabble over who was going to race the quad bike beside the shed to wake up their friends.

9. No matter what the quality of your jeans is, you should wash them in cold water before you wear them, just in case they shrink.

10. Warren wanted to watch the soccer squad do squats and other exercises before the game started.

11. The poodle wagged its tail as it swallowed the fudge that hadn't been washed off the floor in the kitchen.

Real words: (oa) and (oe) Sounds

Tutors

Often, when 2 vowels are together, either the first vowel is sounded and the second is silent, or the first vowel is silent and the second is sounded. Sometimes they do not say either vowel sound. An (oa) says 1. Long vowel (o), as in *boat,* as the (a), is silent. 2. (or), as in *broad* and *soar.* The (oe) says 1. Long vowel (o), as in *toe.* 2. Long (oo), as in *shoe* and *canoe.* 3. Short (u), as in *does,* as the vowel (o), can say the short (u) sound.

Read: (oa) and (oe) Sounds

boat	croak	toaster
toe	boar	boast
does	oars	hoarse
goal	groan	woe
goes	roast	coarse
road	shoe	boasted
soap	toad	Joan
poem	foe	throat
roar	Joe	coast
foam	coach	broad
soar	board	roasted
soak	toes	cupboard
doe	moan	canoes

Spell

Tutors

Remind students that they must listen to which sound makes sense, e.g. Is it a long vowel (o) or the (or) sound, in *board?* An (oe) says 1. Long (o), as in *toe.* 2. Long (oo), as in *shoe.* 3. Short (u), as in *does.* Encourage the student to use their strategies to work out unknown words. Re-read sentences that do not make sense or if errors have been made.

Ask questions, e.g. No. 4. Why did Joe have a smile on his face? No. 8. Where do you find lions in the wild?

Read

1. The children were hoping that the tiny foal would not step on their toes or their shoes as it went into the horse float.

2. Joan will cook the bread in the toaster and butter it on the chopping board before she sits down to eat her breakfast.

3. The sisters had sore throats and they moaned and groaned all day until they all went to visit their doctor in the afternoon.

4. Joe had a broad smile on his face when he arrived at the coast with his board and saw the huge waves crashing onto the beach.

5. The boar loved to wallow and soak in the mud because it made him cool and no insects could sting him.

6. People were moaning as they waited in line for a long time to have a feast of roast meat and vegetables.

7. The surfboard floated away from the edge of the shore, so Warren took his canoe and oars to bring it back.

8. There was an uproar when people found out that the poacher did not moan when he found the roaring lion under the netting.

9. The cheer squad moaned and groaned as their throats were hoarse from screaming at their friends, at the soccer match.

10. We put soap into the warm water to make foam so that we could soak our clothes and towels before washing them.

11. An eagle is a foe of stoats and weasels; therefore, they need to hide when huge birds soar in the sky looking for food to eat.

Real Words: (ou), (ough), (gh) Sounds

Read: (ou), (ough), (gh) Sounds

our	tour	through
out	youth	ghetto
about	around	tourist
shout	found	bounce
you	though	proud
house	double	thought
your	amount	brought
mouse	trouble	noun
round	bought	mountain
four	gherkin	fountain
soup	sound	country
group	fought	touch
cloud	enough	couple

Spell

Sentences: (ou), (ough) and (gh) Sounds

Read

1. The newspaper told us about the four German tourists who went missing while climbing a mountain in France.

2. "You should double that number when you get your answer to four groups of fourteen," the teacher explained to the children.

3. The tour manager thought that they should have enough tourists to take a voyage on a boat, as well as go through a mountain pass on a train.

4. The conductor won't have enough sheets of music for the concert as a couple of them fell into the water in a fountain.

5. A couple of children thought that they saw a ball bounce through the crowd and into a stream that ran through the city.

6. People didn't have trouble seeing a large number of houses on South Beach, as they were painted with yellow and white stripes.

7. A group of about four children were very proud when they found a couple of seals swimming in their pool at school.

8. In nineteen forty, thousands of men and women from Greece and France fought with New Zealanders and Australians, in a war.

9. The teacher shook with fear when a ghastly mouse ran across the lounge floor and hid in the young boy's bag.

10. A couple of young men and their friends had trouble removing a booklet that they had found floating in a deep, round tank.

11. The young man wound the bandage around the wound on his leg because he found that it helped to stop the bleeding and to lessen the pain.

Real Words: (oy) and (oi) Sounds

Tutors

The (oy) in *toy* and *soil* says the same sound. Never use (oi) at the end of a word. The (oy) can be used at the beginning, middle or end of a word.

Remind the student of the syllable division rules if necessary. Other words with the (ay) sound have been added to ensure that the student is looking carefully at the letters of the word and not guessing.

Read: (oy) and (oi) Sounds

boy	essay	enjoyment
toy	point	Troy
day	joint	clay
oil	joyful	today
toil	choice	royal
play	dismay	pointer
foil	spoiled	loyal
enjoy	employ	appoint
coin	destroy	moisture
played	annoy	display
joy	relay	soya
enjoyed	noisy	oyster
avoid	poison	ointment

Spell

Sentences: (oy) and (oi) Sounds

Tutors

Remind the student of the two ways of writing the (oy) sound. An (oy) can be used at the beginning, middle or end of a word, and (oi) is never used at the end of a word.

Remember to ask questions, e.g. No. 4. Why would they be afraid of sharks? No. 5. Why should you get a snake catcher to remove the snake? No. 6. What poisoned the toe?

Read

1. Marks had spoiled our clothes from clay and soil, so we had to wash them in soap and boiling water to get them clean.

2. Joan and Joe got a lot of enjoyment from only paying a gold coin to join the Royal School of Puppets.

3. Could you appoint a leader to take these noisy children into the concert hall to see the play called, "A Voyage to the Moon"?

4. It was our choice to join our mates who were swimming in the lake so that we would avoid the white pointer shark at the beach.

5. A black snake was coiled around the branch of the tree and it was our choice to employ a snake catcher to remove it for us.

6. We had an appointment at the doctors to get ointment for the toe that had been poisoned by a spider.

7. Troy was appointed to carry the silver medals to the mint to be boiled down into coins for my family to enjoy.

8. People from Greece, France and Spain were employed to teach children how to do the royal dances of their countries.

9. The squad of soccer players were annoyed when their food was spoiled and had to be destroyed.

10. Joy joined her friends who were overjoyed at the thought of having the choice between a voyage on a ship or an old steamboat.

11. The moisture from the rain helped to wash the oysters that were on the rocks. Some had been poisoned and destroyed by the hot weather.

Read: (or), (ore), (our), (oar), (oor), (ough), (war) and (ar) Sounds

your	sport	order
short	board	floor
before	score	chore
form	ward	wharf
warm	shark	yourself
mark	poor	regard
boar	north	torched
store	bought	fought
morning	storm	fork
forty	warn	harbour
farm	thought	tore
pour	soar	fourteen
sore	born	corner

Spell

Tutors

Remind the student that (R) and (W) can control vowel sounds. Verbally model how to chunk longer words into syllables.

Ask questions, e.g. No. 5. What is a lark? No. 6. What harmed the city? No. 10. Why could the children be hungry?

Read

1. I bought a horse before I moved to the country, so for a short time, I had to store its food on the floor of our garage.

2. The police had to warn the children that a couple of people had seen sharks swimming offshore during the morning; therefore, all, not part of the beach was closed.

3. I bought food from the store, as it was my chore to feed forty newborn chickens before I went to school in the morning.

4. A swarm of bees stung the poor old horse, so he was put in a barn and brought a cart of food to enjoy.

5. Enjoy yourself as you sit in the warm sun on the farmhouse porch and listen to the larks as they fly and sing in the sky above the backyard.

6. In the last big war, about fourteen ships that were tied up at a wharf in a harbour were torched and destroyed by bombs.

7. We had scratches all over our arms because we had to ward off branches of thorns, as we marched beside some trees on sports day.

8. We brought forty students to watch the eagle soar above the store in the morning sun.

9. The car honked its horn to warn people that the ducklings were crossing the road by the corner of a pond.

10. As a reward for cleaning up after the storm, Fred ordered forty more tarts for the starving children to enjoy.

11. We thought that the score from the sports team was quite poor, but all they needed was more food at halftime to perform better.

12. We had to nail the new boards onto the floor of the storeroom by the harbour, as the storm had damaged them.

Real Words: Multisyllabic Words

Tutor

Multisyllabic words have more than two syllables. When breaking these words into syllables, use the same rules as you would for open, closed and irregular syllable words, e.g. *be/gin/ning, con/so/nant, div/i/ded*. The number of vowel sounds will equal the number of syllables. Get the student to put their hand under their jaw to feel the syllables. Start working from the first vowel sounds in each word and work along the word.

The student can use a pencil or use a finger to chunk each syllable, moving the pencil or finger along the word in syllables, if they are not confident enough to do without these. If a word does not sound right when saying the word using the long vowel sound, try the short sound and listen to which word sounds right, e.g. *mo/del/ling* or *mod/el/ling*.

Refer to the page that explains syllable divisions to revise the rules for dividing words, if necessary.

Read: Multisyllabic Words

adventure	disappear	computer
patterning	consonant	enjoyment
deducted	confusing	understand
ambulance	beginning	travelling
celebrate	determine	detergent
lemonade	atomic	represent
reference	different	boundary
elected	inhabit	gradual
reflected	dinosaur	excellent
rapidly	tornado	absolute
history	seventy	vitamin
illustrate	chimpanzee	modelling

Spell

Read

1. It is often confusing for older people or beginners learning how to use a computer to know that the start symbol is used to begin and end a session.

2. It is beginning to blow because a tornado is travelling towards the city and it could demolish many houses.

3. Seventy, beautiful birds that were imported from different countries had different patterns of feathers on their bodies.

4. When you use detergent and boiling water to clean a frying pan or dirty dishes, all of the greases will rapidly disappear.

5. At the beginning of the storm, there was a gradual rise in the wind speed, and then it rapidly increased until it was almost a tornado.

6. A dinosaur is from history but chimpanzees can be found in the wilderness, in many zoos and can also be seen performing in some circus shows.

7. Can you calculate the difference between a rectangle and a prism's area because when you have finished, you need to draw a line of symmetry through each?

8. A popular or common flower that grows in a state or country is often used as the emblem to represent that place.

9. The discovery of vandals breaking someone's belongings can disappoint anyone, no matter where they live.

10. There was an argument between a teenager and her friends because one wanted a lemonade drink and the other wanted a refreshing orange juice.

11. We remembered that a crocodile had been discovered in the muddy stream last winter, so nobody wanted to go swimming in that river.

Real words: (er), (ir), (ur), (wor), (ear), (our), (re) and (yr) Sounds

Tutors

The (er), is an R controlled vowel. The (R) changes the sound of the vowel. The (er) sound is a homophone as it sounds the same, but it is spelt differently, e.g. 1. (er), as in *fern*. 2. (ir), as in *girl*. 3. (ur), as in *turn*. 4. (wor), as in *word*. 5. (ear), as in *early*. 6. (our), as in *journey*. 7. (re), as in *litre*. 8. (yr), as in *myrtle*.

The (er), particularly at the end of a word, can say the short vowel (u) sound and is called a *schwa* sound, which linguistically is an unaccented vowel sound. Every vowel has a schwa sound and is different in every English dialect.

Read: (er), (ir), (ur), (wor), (ear), (our), (re) and (yr) Sounds

girl	sister	thirteen
fern	birth	chirp
term	Perth	theatre
learn	purple	labour
metre	centre	journey
myrtle	pearl	purse
nurse	shirt	journal
surf	litre	thirsty
early	colour	kilometre
verb	murmur	dirty
third	merge	thermos
herd	flavour	mermaid
ever	nursery	acre

Spell

Sentences: (er), (ir), (ur), (wor), (our), (ear), (re) and (yr) Sounds

Tutors

Remind the student that (R) controlled vowels have a unique sound. Put the sounds onto a flash card and often revise, if the student finds it difficult to recall the phoneme's sounds, automatically. Help them to divide the words into syllables if they have difficulties and remind them of the rules that apply to those words.

Ask questions, e.g. No. 5. Why is the word *nursery* used in this sentence? What is a journey?

Read

1. After a long search for the turtle, which was worth a lot of money, it was found on the edge of the kerb by the fountain.

2. We measure liquids by the litre and length by the metre, so go and write in words how much string will be needed to go around the twenty-litre jar.

3. The tree fern has brown, curly fronds emerging from the centre which will turn into different coloured green leaves, the same colour as a myrtle tree.

4. The boy should go to the swimming pool early tomorrow morning to search for the yellow and purple striped shirt that he left there after sports day.

5. Some birds will journey many kilometres to make a nest, lay eggs and have a nursery full of chirping babies to feed worms.

6. A turnip grows in soil from the earth, so wash off the dirt before you cut it up and turn it into soup for dinner.

7. You and your teacher will be very proud of your exam results and agree that all of the hard work of pursuing long hours of study, earned you great rewards.

8. I heard of a person who went to Perth to research the journey of two of our world's planets, Jupiter and Mercury, to see if they travel around the Earth.

9. The new purple ice cream was the worst of all the flavours to eat, as it was quite bitter and sour, so nobody ever repurchased it.

10. The diver dived into the sea in search of pearls from oysters and then he brought them to the surface where there was no pounding surf.

11. Thirteen, thirsty girls wanted their friends to squirt cool water into their mouths, as they had just finished a long, thirty kilometres journey, on foot.

Real Words: (au) and (aw) Sounds

Tutors

The (au) and (aw) phonemes can say (or); however, (au) can say other sounds as well. The (au) says 1. Long vowel (a), as in *gauge*. 2. Long vowel (u), as in *beauty*. 3. Short vowel (o), as in *Australia*. 4. (ar) sound, as in *aunt* and *laugh*. 5. (or), as in *taught*. 6. (arf), as in *laugh*. When students pronounce a word and it does not sound right, ask them to try another sound that the phoneme can make, i.e. *flip* the sound, until the word makes sense.

Depending on the accent of a country, *because* can be pronounced by saying the (au), as a short vowel (o) or as an (or) sound. Remind the student to chunk longer words into syllables.

Read: (au) and (aw) Sounds

because	laugh	strawberry
dinosaur	audit	assault
crawl	drawn	tawny
Australia	lawn	fault
cause	caustic	authority
Paul	audio	authentic
August	sauce	sausage
hawk	claw	crawled
aunty	gauge	laundry
pause	autumn	naughty
haul	author	squawking
prawn	Austria	automatic

Spell

Tutors

Remind the student of the sounds that (au) and (aw) can make. They should listen to whether the word makes sense in the context of the sentence and try another sound if the word does not sound right. Model how to chunk multisyllabic words into syllables. Re-read sentences that have errors in them to practise the unknown words or put them on a card to revise and learn.

Ask questions, No. 6. What does "exhausted" mean? No. 8. What are the two meanings for *poor, that* could be used in this sentence? No. 9. Where would the artist be drawing his picture?

Read

1. An author wrote about the differences between the sharks and dinosaurs that were on display in an Australian museum.

2. Paul had auburn coloured hair that matched the autumn leaves which were on the lawn by the pile of sawdust.

3. Don't let that hawk taunt the South Australian parrot in its cage, as the effect of the trauma could cause the parrot to fret and die.

4. In August, it is autumn in Austria, so you can see many people sprawled all over lawns enjoying the warm, sunny days.

5. Some cooks from Australia and Austria made authentic meals out of prawns and sausages, followed by strawberries and cream.

6. A small boy was exhausted because he had to haul loads of laundry in his rickshaw, from dawn to dusk, to make enough money to buy food for his family.

7. An assault on a person can be daunting and cause traumas later in life; therefore, tell someone who works for the law, like a policeman, about what happened.

8. My poor aunt, who was wrapped in a shawl, flaunted her expensive jewellery and caused some people to wonder where she had got it all from.

9. The young artist had drawn a picture of the exhaust pipes that were coming out of the back of fishing trawlers and a launch, that was tied up at a wharf.

10. The automatic washing machine in the laundry had a fault in its electrics, as someone had dropped caustic soda and sauce all over the motor.

11. The sauce for the sausages spilled over the prawns that were cooking on the barbecue.

Read: (ar), (are) and (aer) Sounds

part	hare	aerobatics
farm	partly	snare
care	glare	starch
darn	parents	aerosol
harp	harm	vary
bare	rare	remark
dare	spark	regarded
farmer	lark	voluntary
aerate	stare	commentary
Mary	aeroplane	aerofoil
shark	aerial	apartment
fare	started	necessary
March	spare	area

Spell

Sentences: (ar), (are) and (aer) Sounds

Read

1. Mary and her parents went to an apartment by the beach for a barbeque and pool party for the first birthday of her cousin, Mark.

2. The aeroplane did aerobatic movements in the sky, then darted towards a pole and scared all of the spectators.

3. A new program came onto the market, so it was necessary to restart the computer for an automatic upgrade.

4. Many people stared at the huge aerial on the back of a fast car, as it started to make noises that caused all the dogs to bark loudly.

5. The farmer had to put the spare wheel on his tractor, as he ran over a broken jar that was partly hidden in the grass and punctured a tyre.

6. We listened to a commentary about Australian aerobatic racers who did daring flight movements under large bridges and over low areas of farmland.

7. The farmer had a spare garage in the backyard, near the barn of his old homestead, so that he could take care of all his vintage cars.

8. You need to be very wary of animals that can harm you, like sharks and bears, and be on guard when you are in the areas where they live.

9. In March, spectators were scared when they watched a man from Austria do daring aerobatic twists and turns in his aeroplane before he darted towards the finish line.

10. My parents told me not to be scared of the sharks in a large tank when I went to a birthday party at Underwater World.

11. The glare from the beautiful, sparkling water was quickly darkened as a cloud partly covered the sun.

Real Words: (igh), (eigh), (ough) and (augh) Sounds

Tutors

A (gh) is silent after a vowel; therefore, (igh), says a long (i), as in *right*. An (eigh) says a long vowel (a) sound, as in *eight*. An (ough) says 1. Long vowel (o), as in *though*. 2. (or), as in *thought*. 3. (uff), as in *enough*. 4. (off), as in *cough*. An (augh) says 1. (or), as in *caught*. 2. (arf), as in *laugh*.

Remind the student of how to divide a longer word into syllables. If the word does not sound right, ask the student to try another sound that the phoneme makes, until the word makes sense.

Read: (igh), (eigh), (ough) and (augh) Sounds

right	though	fought
eight	weigh	freight
caught	enough	laughter
brought	cough	sleigh
tighter	neigh	thoughtful
frighten	straight	lightest
taught	knight	enlighten
thought	slightly	highway
dough	daughter	delightful
weight	midnight	neighbour
bought	tough	straighter
bright	naughty	haughty
nought	laugh	rough

Spell

Sentences: (igh), (eigh), (ough) and (augh) Sounds

Tutors

Remind the student of the sounds and rules of these phonemes. Read as many sentences as desired in one session.

Ask questions, e.g. No.1. What could have caused the accident? No. 4. Why might the nurses be eating after midnight?

Read

1. The accident at the traffic lights on the highway happened at midnight and the ambulance took the lady straight to a hospital to treat her for the shock.

2. We thought it was tough for the heavy person to walk on a tightrope but when they brought out a lighter person, we all began to laugh with delight.

3. Please enlighten me on how that naughty pony cut her thigh and almost got knocked over by a freight truck on the highway.

4. After finishing a night shift of nursing, our nightly ritual at midnight was to go to the kitchen to eat honey on bread.

5. Our neighbour had brought enough money to buy his daughter a delightful little puppy that was the lightest weight of the litter.

6. Although we thought Lewis was pretending to be ill by coughing, he had caught a virus, so we took him straight to the doctor.

7. Mary taught her daughter to be thoughtful towards her neighbours, by not frightening them with loud laughter after midnight.

8. Because the dough did not have enough milk in it, the bread was very tough to eat, so the baker thought that he should put slightly more milk in the mixture, the next time he baked.

9. All of the traffic on the highway was caught up in a traffic jam that was backed up at the railway crossing because the freight train was slightly late.

10. My daughter shouted with delight as she caught an ocean liner to take her on an eighteen-day journey around eight countries.

11. The trucks carried freight down the highway. The weight of the loads caused the roads to become rough and broken; therefore, they needed to be repaired.

Real Words: (ey) Sounds

Tutor

There are two sounds for (ey) 1. Long vowel (a), as in *they*. 2. Long vowel (e), as in *key*. If the (e) sound does not sound right, *flip* over to the (a) sound. We need to make meaning when reading texts; therefore, words and sentences must make sense.

The (ay) phoneme has been added so that the student looks carefully at the letters and does not guess words. Assist them with chunking and verbally model how to split a word into syllables, if necessary.

Read: (ey) Sounds

they	grey	hockey
key	kidney	chimney
money	trolley	surveying
hey	monkey	obeyed
honey	survey	osprey
obey	parsley	turkey
clay	display	disobey
valley	barley	storey
spray	jockey	playful
prey	chutney	journey
alley	stray	motley
donkey	convey	crayfish
jersey	Abbey	attorney

Spell

Read

1. We found eggs beside an empty osprey's nest on top of a fourteen-storey apartment, so we put them into an incubator to see if they would hatch.

2. It was cold as Abbey pushed her trolley down the alley between the shops, so she had to put on her grey jersey.

3. We required lots of money to buy expensive hockey sticks for the representative teams so that they could score goals to win their games.

4. The old donkey went on a journey with its owner to buy honey, barley and parsley, so that the cook could make a tasty meal for dinner.

5. If you disobey your surgeon and eat that hot chutney, you could damage your kidneys and liver and then he will have to operate on you, again.

6. Yesterday, we saw a graceful osprey flying over the sparkling water down in the valley, as it was looking for prey to eat.

7. Little Miss Muffet was very disappointed to eat curds and whey because the turkey came and devoured all of her breakfast.

8. The developer wanted to survey some land for his new building, so he had to wait a fortnight and then pay a lot of money to get the key for the block of old apartments that he wanted to demolish.

9. The monkey was riding a motley coloured donkey like a jockey in the story, "A Journey from Turkey to Greece."

10. Hey, you speak like a cockney from London; therefore, if you want to convey your message to your listeners, you will need to talk slowly to them.

11. Abbey, an attorney, loved to watch the grey osprey soar in the valley as it hunted its prey in the river and out at sea.

Real words: Rule 4. (i) in a Multisyllabic Word

Tutors

The vowel (i) can stand at the end of a syllable and give its short vowel sound when it is either unaccented or used as a connective vowel, e.g. *at/ti/tude*. When you divide a syllable after the internal (i), it will usually say a short (i) sound.

Divide multisyllabic words, as for closed, open or irregular syllables. Allow the student to use their finger or pencil to chunk a longer word into its syllables if they are not confident dividing syllables. Every syllable has a vowel sound in it.

Read: Rule 4. (i) in a multisyllabic word

family	principal	quality
visitor	possible	aquarium
difficult	competitive	attitude
qualify	quantity	sacrifice
gravity	deliberate	principle
centimetre	physical	magistrate
accident	policy	Madison
activity	consider	continent
horrify	monitor	invisible
diligent	specific	responsible
unify	delivery	repetitive
resident	humility	vaccinate
positive	visibility	responsibility

Spell

Read

1. Madison and Andrew thought that they had caused the accident on a computer and found it difficult to explain to the principal what had happened. He was horrified to learn that the monitor had been broken when it was delivered; therefore, they were not responsible for the damage.

2. Mr Lewis needed to be vaccinated so that his physical health did not suffer as he regularly visited the residents of poor villages in Africa, on a repetitive basis. His family doctor thought that he would qualify for being injected with a vaccine, every time he flew to the continent of Africa.

3. The magistrate did not like the attitude of people who deliberately did acts of violence on the streets. He asked for police officers to monitor every activity that occurred in the streets every night, to ensure that visitors did not stay away from their town.

4. Some competitors found it challenging to make the Olympic Games teams. They had to be diligent in their long hours of training and be very responsible for sacrificing junk food so that they could keep their bodies in peak form for their best performances. Many were disappointed when they were told that they had not made a team.

5. Many pupils had to learn the principle that when things fall, it is a result of gravity. It is impossible to see gravity, but it is possible to look at the results of this theory. We need to experiment with this theory to prove it is correct.

6. An accident occurred several centimetres away from the highway's traffic lights at midnight. The ambulance took the person straight to the hospital so that the doctors could evaluate whether they needed to be admitted overnight. The police were investigating the incident.

7. Residents of houses in some European countries need to build high-quality buildings, as they need to consider climatic conditions like freezing snow in winter to intense heat in summer.

Read: (ui) and (ue) Sounds

fruit	argue	dialogue
suit	avenue	tissue
build	bruise	pursue
guitar	circuit	pursuit
clue	guilt	recruit
venue	building	rebuilt
juice	issue	guinea-pig
true	cruise	analogue
fuel	vogue	nuisance
biscuit	catalogue	revenue
guide	tongue	barbecue
vague	guilty	plague
built	statue	penguin

Spell

Read

1. Vague clues eventuated during a dialogue between the police officers and the public, but eventually, a lead was provided, which led to the boys in blue being in pursuit of the offenders who had stolen the motorbike.

2. A plague of fruit flies infested our lemon and orange trees; therefore, we had no suitable fruit to make juice to drink for breakfast.

3. Sue played her guitar and sang songs on a cruise ship, as a way of raising revenue to pay for her university studies.

4. The army recruits were guided to a statue where they were required to build a tower and climb to the top of it, to display their fitness and strength.

5. There was an issue at a concert when a contestant could not get her tongue around the name of the venue she was at, in Prague.

6. The father penguin jumped into the freezing water in pursuit of fish to bring back to his starving, young chick.

7. The guinea-pig was a nuisance, as he not only ate all of our vegetables and fruit in the garden but also damaged all of the flowers.

8. The salesman was vague about whether the price of the guitar included the cost of the case; therefore, the boy was unsure if he had raised enough money to buy it.

9. The history of the statue was etched into the stone of a plaque and then placed in front of the Parliament Buildings.

10. You cannot argue about the fact that nine o'clock at night in analogue time is the same as twenty-one hours in digital time, in the evening.

11. On the front cover of the latest issue of Vogue magazine, there was a young model dressed in a striking blue suit.

Real Words: (ie) and (ei) Sounds

Tutors

An (ie) says 1. Long vowel (e), as in *thief*. 2. Short vowel (i), as in *sieve*. 3. Long vowel (i), as in *pie*. 4. Short vowel (e), as in *friend*. An (ei) says 1. Long vowel (e), as in *receive* and *seize*. 2. Long vowel (a), as in *vein*. 3. Short vowel (i), as in *forfeit*. A sentence that can help learn a general rule of the spelling of the (ie) and (ei) words is: *(i) before (e) except after (c),* as in *receive*. However, there are exceptions to this rule and this sentence can be learnt to assist with remembering some of these: *Neither foreign sovereign seized the counterfeited and forfeited leisure.*

When (ie) is in a suffix (ier), (ied) and (ies), the (ie) will say either a long vowel (e) or (i), depending on the root word, e.g. 1. *Silly* changes to *sillier*, a long vowel (e) sound. 2. *Dry* changes to *dried*, a long vowel (i). 3. *City* changes to *cities*, a long vowel (e) sound. Always remind students to listen to the word and ask themselves," Does that make sense?" then try the other sound that the phoneme can make.

Read: (ie) and (ei) Sounds

thief	seize	weight
denies	grief	field
dried	deceive	niece
cities	neither	reins
receive	receipt	conceive
brief	belief	relief
vein	piece	satisfied
friend	applies	grieve
briefly	studied	neighbour
ceiling	chief	terrified
either	veil	achieve

Spell

Plural means more than one. Apply these rules to make plurals. 1. A word ending with (y), change the (y) to (i) and add (es), e.g. *city* becomes *cities*. 2. A word ending in (f), change the (f) to (v) and add (es), e.g. *thief* becomes *thieves*. Roof is an exception, *roofs.*

Read

1. Our neighbour's friend had an awful accident, and she broke her arm and cut a vein near her wrist. We phoned the ambulance and she received help to relieve the terrible pain before she arrived at the hospital.

2. There was a brief calm in the storm and we received some relief from the pounding rain of the cyclone, but we were terrified when the gale force winds began again, after the eye of the storm passed over.

3. My niece achieved excellent marks in her dance performance and was relieved to know she had passed the exam and would be receiving a certificate. She had studied hard and was satisfied and relieved that neither she nor her friend had failed the exam.

4. The students applied themselves diligently to their studies at university to achieve a degree in science. They believed that their research would eventually enable them to work, either in food hygiene or weight control.

5. A piece of rein broke on the bridle and the rider of the horse was terrified as the horse tried to jump a fence in the field. Fortunately, a shriek from an angry magpie defending its territory, scared the horse and it ran to the neighbour's house; therefore, neither horse nor rider was hurt.

6. You can hang material like a wedding veil from your ceiling to protect yourself against mosquitoes, or you can spray insecticide in the room so that you can get some relief from the pests. Only give a brief spray as many people believe that it is not healthy for you.

7. A thief seized some counterfeit bank notes and tried to deceive some foreigners by using them to buy goods. Fortunately, some local people received a warning in the daily news and the police arrested eight people. All of the locals received a reward from the chief of police.

Real Words: (tion) and (sion) Sounds

Tutors

The (ti) and (si) phonemes say (sh). A (tion) says (shon), as in *addition*. A (sion) says 1. (shon), as in se*ssion*. 2. (zon), as in *division*. There is never a (cion), as (ci) says (si). The words *fashion* and *cushion*, are exceptions to this rule and the (sh) says its name in the middle of each word.

Remind the students of how to divide multisyllabic words.

Read: (tion) and (sion) Sounds

addition	fusion	dictionary
subtraction	competition	mansion
session	condition	relation
division	decision	cushion
multiplication	vision	evaluation
instruction	delusion	partition
action	collection	domination
question	confusion	concession
pension	mission	occupation
nation	prescription	duplication
caution	fashion	permission
motion	conversation	satisfaction
tension	discussion	revision

Spell

Tutors

Remind students that (tion), says *shon* and (sion), says *shon* or *zon*. Verbally model how to chunk multisyllabic words into syllables, if this is needed.

Ask questions, e.g. No. 4. Why would they need to use caution when finding the total? No. 5. What is an interpreter? No. 6. What does permission mean?

Read

1. The teacher had illustrations and explanations in her lesson to try to convince her students that division was the opposite of multiplication. In the next lesson, the students asked questions and achieved a better understanding of the concept.

2. Before a gymnastic competition, all of the competitors were given instructions on how points would be deducted for inappropriate actions before their final marks were announced. The judge then gave a demonstration, with illustrations, about what these actions were, to all of the gymnasts.

3. The mansion would be built beside the river on the condition that the owner checked that the floods would not cause any destruction to their property. A duplication of this report needed to be sent to engineers and councillors.

4. "Can you weigh our collection of vegetables and use a calculator to add up how much money we will receive for the products? Please use caution when using addition and multiplication to receive your total," explained the teacher.

5. There was confusion between two customers from two different counties when they were having a conversation about their different lifestyles. This conversation had many complications, which turned into an argument; therefore, we had to get an interpreter to cease all communication between them.

6. I received permission to calm an anxious person who was to receive an award for her excellent description of being terrified in a theme park. I did achieve satisfaction when we both began to laugh about a few events, which calmed her nerves.

7. I was worried that I would miss my final exam because I had to ask for permission to quickly change out of my dirty, sweaty clothes from my rugby competition and change into fancier, cleaner clothes.

8. We needed to take quick action to get permission to have a fashion show in a month's time. There were many discussions and decisions to be made, to find out how many articles of clothing would be required for the event.

Real Words: (cian), (cial), (tial) and (ive) Sounds

Tutors

The (ci) and (ti) phonemes say (sh). 1. A (cian) says *shan*, as in *optician*. 2. A (cial) says *shall*, as in *special*. 3. A (tial) says *shall*, as in *initial*. 4. A (sian) says *zan*, as in *Asian*.

Because (v) is always spelt with an (e), at the end of a word, as in *live*, the vowel can say either its long or short vowel sounds. The (ive) words have been added here to ensure that the student is looking carefully at all of the letters of a word and not guessing. Verbally model to the student how to chunk words into syllables, if they are having difficulties.

Read: (cian), (cial), (tial) and (ive) Sounds

special	politician	assertive
social	initial	explosive
active	attractive	potentially
facial	especially	suggestive
positive	magician	electrician
official	relative	initially
spatial	musician	incentive
negative	potential	tactician
racial	destructive	specially
expensive	imaginative	objective
essential	dietician	impressive
partial	martial	paediatrician
torrential	beautician	Asian

Spell

Sentences: (cian), (cial), (tial) and (ive) Sounds

Tutors

Remind the student the (ci) and (ti) say a (sh) sound. Model how to chunk words into syllables if the student is struggling with multisyllabic words. Read as many sentences as desired. Never push the student or frustrate them, as they can lose heart and give up trying. Praise every effort.

Ask questions, e.g. No. 4. What were the students' interests? No. 6. Why would it be essential to have an electrician to wire up the instruments?

Read

1. A selective group of musicians were to receive an award for their rendition of the National Anthem. The official winners would receive an expensive dinner to enjoy the celebration with some of the other competitors.

2. It is essential for all officials and competitors of a sport to remain positive, especially in competitions, so that each competitor can display their potential in a game. The officials and players will receive tremendous applause at the end of the tournament if their team wins.

3. An apprentice electrician had the potential of causing a destructive fire when he accidentally crossed the negative and positive wires. Luckily, an official from the electricity department did an inspection and rectified the confusion.

4. There was to be a partial blackout of the moon; therefore, some students decided to study lunar eclipses. They had the potential of becoming astronauts, but it would be an expensive occupation to study at university.

5. In big ocean races, yachts require a tactician and very energetic sailors. All of those who had the potential of being selected for these positions had to have a special interview and fitness test.

6. An electrician was required to wire up the musicians' instruments to prevent a potential fire from occurring. A destructive fire could cause a massive disaster, especially if there are to be thousands of people watching the concert.

7. A dietician suggests a selection of food for sick people to eat. It is essential that they follow these suggestions, as there will be a negative effect on their health if they don't and then they will probably receive a caution from their doctor.

8. A politician from an Asian country gave expensive musical instruments to some poorer countries so that some children could achieve their dreams and visions of producing amazing music and entering lots of worldwide competitions.

Real Words: (ous), (cious), (tious) and (xious) Sounds

Tutors

1. An (ous) says (us), as in *joyous*. 2. (tious) and (cious) say *shus*, as in *cautious* and *spacious*. 3. (xious) says *zus*, as in *anxious*, as (x) says (z) at the beginning of a word, as in *xylophone*.

As there are multisyllabic words, help the student to chunk words into syllables, according to the rules they have learnt.

Read: (ous), (cious), (tious) and (xious) Sounds

serious	vigorous	continuous
cautious	delicious	noxious
obvious	suspicious	courteous
famous	hilarious	gracious
anxious	ingenious	glamorous
callous	vicious	spacious
joyous	rigorous	tremendous
precious	ingeniously	obnoxious
various	luscious	graciously
envious	vigorously	outrageous
wondrous	vivacious	pretentious
nervous	callously	scandalous
marvellous	porous	precarious

Spell

Sentences: (ous), (cious), (tious) and (xious) Sounds

Tutors

An (ous) says (*us*), as in *joyous*. Remind the students that (tious) and (cious), say *shus* and the (xious) says *zus,* because (x) can say (z). As there are multisyllabic words, help the student to chunk words into syllables, according to the rules they have learnt.

Ask questions, e.g. No. 1. What could happen to sailors who don't listen to instructions? No. 2. Who ordered the special meals? No. 6. What does vicious mean?

Read

1. Your spatial awareness is essential when you are a tactician or sailor on a yacht that is not very spacious. Vigorous sailors continuously receive orders, so it is critical that they are cautious and listen carefully to all instructions so that a serious disaster does not happen.

2. The dietician ordered special meals of selective foods for a patient under the recommendation of the doctor. These meals were quite expensive, but they were delicious and made others envious of the luscious meals.

3. The politicians ordered martial law when a destructive earthquake caused confusion and panic amongst the residents in the city; therefore, they had a partial closure of the city and the police arrested any suspicious looters.

4. The facial expressions of the judges showed how gracious they were, especially when one competitor was obnoxious and had no manners. Anyway, they put their initials on the award to prove how courteous they were.

5. There was a famous swimmer who had the potential of becoming a hilarious comedian, but he was too nervous to go on stage. However, some ingenious person suggested that he become a glamorous model.

6. A callous thief stole a pensioner's wheelchair, so a collection was taken by the public to raise money to buy another one. He graciously thanked everyone on television for their generous donations and he also forgave the vicious attacker.

7. If you are serious about being fit, you will need to do rigorous exercises when you are training for a sport. You will receive tremendous rewards, especially if you have to do a whole day of competitions.

8. We were very nervous when the wind from the hurricane vigorously blew the fruit trees. It was quite obvious that many of the delicious mangoes would be ruined when they dropped to the ground.

Real Words: Silent Letters

Tutors

There are many silent letters: 1. (kn) says (n), as in *know*. 2. (wr) says (r), as in *write*. 3. (mb) says (m), as in *climb*. 4. (sc), says (s), as in *scissors*. 5. (dge) says (j), as in *bridge*. 6. (gn) says (n), as in *sign*. 7. (mn) says (m), as in *autumn*. 8. (pn) says (n), as in *pneumonia*. 9. (ps) says (s), as in *psalm*. 10. (is) says long (i), as in *island*. 11. (l) is silent in: *could, calf, chalk* and *calm*. 12. (h) is silent in: *vehicle, honour, hour, ache, school, ghetto, yoghurt, rhyme* and *when*. 13. (w) is silent in *who, wrap* and *answer*. 14. (t) is silent in: *fetch, soften, mortgage* and *castle*. 15. (qu), the (u) is silent and it says (kw), as in *quick*. 16. (rh) *says (r),* as in *rhinoceros*.

When a student sounds out a word, they need to be thinking; Does that make sense? Does that word sound right in the sentence? Try the other sounds that the phoneme can say or what word would sound right.

Read: Silent Letters

climb	honest	half
island	scheme	rhythm
fudge	scene	column
listen	know	answer
thistle	reign	ghastly
gnome	gnarl	science
receipt	rhinoceros	knowledge
cupboard	wrinkle	vehicle
castle	whole	wriggle
nestle	whistle	wholesale
knuckle	psalm	solemn
gnaw	scenic	doubt
plumber	salmon	scenery

Spell

Read

1. We knew that the plumber was an honest man when he told us that the pipes were not wrecked but they were only filled with wrapping papers from sweets. He had to climb down a ghastly dark hole to collect the destructive rubbish.

2. Because of the tension and anxious moments before an examination, the physics teacher postponed the exam. Instead, the students showed their scientific knowledge by doing engineering experiments on a vehicle's ability to climb steep gradients.

3. An autograph of a famous wrestler from the ghetto was displayed so that it could be auctioned to raise money for the Foundation for Under Privileged Children. An enormous amount of money was raised from this auction, which showed how much the community honoured him.

4. Carpenters, electricians and plumbers are required in the construction of buildings. Insurance agents, bank managers and lawyers are also important people involved when selling or buying a property.

5. Noxious weeds and poisonous chemicals can cause unpleasant consequences to our health. We need to ensure that we know how to look after our bodies by being aware of the things that can harm us. Eat healthy food like vegetables, fruit and fish, like salmon.

6. You could see a tremendous amount of damage to buildings and roads in a city after a magnitude eight earthquake. Millions of dollars would need to be spent on the wrecked and damaged infrastructure, to change the scenery of the place, again.

7. Vehicles that were once allowed to travel on an idyllic island were stopped, as they were ruining the scenery. I believe that everyone should study the science of our flora and fauna, to get knowledge on how to save our planet. We will not be able to listen to the whistle of our precious birds if they are extinct.

8. I received a receipt for my scenic cruise around some amazing islands in the South Pacific. A whole lot of my friends wanted to go to Africa to see the white rhinoceros and others wanted to climb mountains and catch salmon in the Canadian Rockies. I know where I would go.

1. **Congratulations**, you have learnt the majority of the English phonemes or sounds, (for all, refer to "Consonants, Vowels, Digraphs and Trigraphs," in the Appendix). You have also learnt strategies for working out unknown words so that you can make meaning from what you have read.

2. If you do not know a word, miss the unknown word and read on to the end of the sentence or until you get the meaning of what the sentence is about, and then re-read the sentence. If you still don't know the word:
   - Blend the letters slowly or sound out the word in syllables
   - Remember that some sounds have more than one sound; therefore, try the other sounds until the word sounds right or makes sense in the sentence
   - Ask yourself; Does that word sound right? Do we say it like that?

3. English is one of the hardest languages to learn as it is made up of other languages. For example, *chef* is a French word; *water* is a Latin word and *spaghetti* is an Italian word.

4. **Homographs** are words that are spelt the same but have different meanings, e.g. He **wound** the bandage around the **wound.** You need to read the sentence first to get the meaning of each word.

5. **Homophones** are words that sound the same but are spelt differently and have different meanings, e.g. Did you **hear** that the **hare** jumped over **here?** Sometimes you need to use the dictionary to look up the meaning of words.

6. There is also more than one way to spell a phoneme, e.g. the (er) sound. We h**ear**d that a g**ir**l called M**yr**tle told a n**ur**se that she had taken a long j**our**ney to get to h**er** w**or**k. When reading words always listen to what makes sense or if we pronounce or say it like that. The spelling of these words can be tricky.

7. Other words have phonemes that have more than one sound, e.g. (ea) has three sounds. The **great** loaf of **bread** was **eaten.** Try all the sounds that the phoneme makes and listen to what words sound right or makes sense in the context of the sentence. Because some phonemes have more than one sound this makes it hard to spell words, so write the words to decide which word seems right, e.g. (jaw, jor, jour) and determine which word is correct.

8. Read, read and read more. If you want to be good at anything you need to practise. Reading empowers us and opens windows into other worlds.

9. Now set goals for your future. Do you want to be an electrician, physician, plumber, psychologist or a scientist to cure pneumonia? A receptionist, personal assistant, a homemaker or something to do with computers? Whatever you choose, do it with excellence, which means, do everything to the best of *your* ability.

Vowels

Vowel: (Aa)

Vowel (a) can say every vowel sound, but it mostly says the short and long vowel sounds. Make students aware of the schwa sounds that the vowel (a) can make. Choose words to illustrate, according to your artistic ability.

To make a flash card, write (a) in the middle of the card and capital (A) at the bottom of the left-hand corner. On the back of the card, rule lines to divide it into 4-8 section, depending on how many sounds you wish the student to know. 1. On the top left-hand side write *hat*, then draw a picture of a hat underneath and on the right side, write short (a), with the symbol (ᴗ) for the short sound above it. 2. Under this, write *plane*, draw a picture and on the right side, write a long (a), with the symbol (-) for the long sound above it. 3. Under this write, (a) usually says (ar), when there is a: *th, s, f,* or *m* sound after it, with the words *path, grass, half,* and *drama,* then write long (ar), on the right side. 4. At the bottom, write *wasp* and draw a picture, and on the right side, write short (o), with the symbol (ᴗ) for the short sound above it.

Vowel (Aa)

Short (a)	Long (a) VCe/Silent (e)	Long (a) Open syllable, when the first syllable is accented	(ar) (a) usually says (ar) when there is an: s, f, th, m sound after it		Short (o) (a) can say a short (o) sound after a (w) sound, also in salt and malt	
at	same	lady	father	grass	was	quad
and	late	lazy	path	drama	want	squad
am	gave	paper	craft	calm	wash	squat
flap	make	later	half	gasp	wasp	salt

(or) The (W) controlled (a) makes the (ar) say (or)		Short (e)		Short (i)	Short (u) When (a) is at the beginning or the end of a word	
ball	war	any	said	cabbage	about	Anna
call	warm	many	says	shortage	around	Lisa
stall	warn	parent	area	luggage	Donna	across

Can you think of words that fit the above patterns? Write them below.

Short (a)		(ar)		Short (e)	
Long (a)		Short (o)		Short (i)	
Long (a)		(or)		Short (u)	

Vowel, (Ee)

Tutor

Vowel (e) has three sounds, but it mostly says the short and long vowel sounds. 1. Short vowel (e), as in *get*. 2. Long vowel (e), a VCe, silent (e), as in *here and* long vowel (e), in an open syllable, when the first syllable is accented, as in *rely*. 3. Short vowel (i), a schwa sound, as in *even*. Choose words to illustrate, according to your artistic ability.

To make a flash card, write (e) in the middle of the card and capital (E) at the bottom of the left-hand corner. On the back, divide the card into 3 sections. 1. On the top left-hand side, write *ten* and underneath write (10) and on the right side, write (e), with the short symbol (◡), above it. 2. In the middle section write *here*, a picture or a sentence, e.g. *I am here*, and on the right side, write (e), with the long symbol (-), above it. 3. In the bottom section write *seven* and write (7) and on the right side, write (i), with the short symbol (◡), above it.

Vowel (Ee)

Short (e)	Long (e) VCe/Silent (e)	Long (e) Open syllable, when the first syllable is accented	Short (i)
get	here	begin	even
men	there	belong	seven
ten	where	beside	enemy
pen	eve	result	pretty
then	theme	return	comedy
when	these	event	vinegar
them	delete	rely	appetite
set	recede	emu	tragedy

Can you think of words that fit the above patterns? Write them below.

Short (e)	Long (e) VCe/Silent (e)	Long (e) Open syllable, when the first syllable is accented	Short (i)

Vowel, (Ii)

Tutors

Vowel (i) has three sounds, but it mostly says the short and long vowel sounds. 1. Short vowel (i), as in _him_. 2. Long vowel (i), a VCe, silent (e), as in _bike_ and long vowel (i), when the first syllable is accented and the (i) is an open syllable, as in _final. 3._ Long vowel (e), a schwa sound, as in _kiwi_. Choose words to illustrate, according to your artistic ability.

To make a flash card, write (i) in the middle of the card and write the capital (I) at the bottom of the left-hand corner. On the back, divide the card into three sections. 1. On the top left-hand side write _six_, write (6) underneath and on the right side, write (i), with the symbol (ᵕ), for a short vowel above it. 2. In the middle write _nine,_ and underneath write (9), on the right side, write (i), with the symbol (-), for a long vowel above it. 3. At the bottom, write _kiwi,_ and draw a picture underneath and on the right side, write (e), with the symbol (-), for a long vowel above it.

Vowel (Ii)

Short (i)	Long (i) VCe/Silent (e)	Long (i) Open syllable when the first syllable is accented	Long (e)
in	like	writer	kiwi
it	bike	China	ski
is	wide	final	taxi
his	hide	iron	radio
him	nine	pilot	piano
sit	mine	tiger	Lisa
bit	fine	primary	studio
six	while	nicer	machine
big	time	diner	police
pig	line	finest	serious

Can you think of words that fit the above patterns? Write them below.

Short (i)	Long (i) VCe/Silent (e)	Long (i) Open syllable when the first syllable is accented	Long (e)

Vowel, (Oo)

Tutors

Vowel (o) has four sounds, but it mostly says the short and long vowel sounds. 1. Short vowel (o), as in _not_. 2. Long vowel (o), a VCe, silent (e), as in _home_ and long vowel (o), when the first syllable is accented and an open syllable, as in _open_. 3. Long (oo), a schwa sound, as in _to_. 4. Short (u), a schwa sound, as in _come_. Choose words to illustrate, according to your artistic ability.

To make a flash card, write (o) in the middle of the card and capital (O) at the bottom of the left-hand corner. On the back, divide the card into four sections. 1. On the top left-hand side write _stop_, draw a picture underneath and on the right side, write (o), with the symbol (ᴜ), for the short sound above it. 2. Under this, write _bone_ or _oval_, draw a picture and on the right side, write (o), with the symbol (-), for the long sound above it. 3. Under this, write _who_ or _grove_, on the right side, long (oo), with the symbol (-), for the long sound above it. 4. At the bottom, write, _love_ and draw a picture, then on the right side, write (u), with the symbol (ᴜ), for the short sound above it.

Vowel (Oo)

Short (o)	Long (o) VCe/Silent (e)	Long (o) Open syllable when the first syllable is accented	Long (oo)	Short (u)
on	home	open	to	come
of	hope	over	do	some
not	bone	obey	who	other
got	rope	oval	whose	mother
hop	note	holy	whom	above
off	nose	photo	grove	son
stop	rose	total	prove	love
dot	those	Tony	move	Monday
hot	wrote	donut	approve	done

Can you think of words that fit the above patterns? Write them below.

Short (o)	Long (o) VCe/Silent (e)	Long (o) Open syllable when the first syllable is accented	Long (oo)	Short (u)

Vowel, (Uu)

Tutors

Vowel (u) has four sounds, but it mostly says the short and long vowel sounds. 1. Short vowel (u), as in *mum*. 2. Long vowel (u), a VCe, silent (e), as in *use* and long vowel (u), when the first syllable is accented and the (u) is an open syllable, as in *July*. 3. Short (oo), a schwa sound, as in *put*. 4. Short (i), a schwa sound, as in *busy*. Choose words to illustrate, according to your artistic ability.

To make a flash card, write (u) in the middle of the card and capital (U) at the bottom of the left-hand corner. On the back, divide the card into four sections. 1. On the top left-hand side write *sun*, draw a picture underneath and on the right side, write (u), with the symbol (ᴗ), for the short sound above it. 2. Under this write *cube,* draw a picture and on the right side, write (u), with the symbol (-), for the long sound above it. 3. Under this write *bush,* draw a picture and on the right side, write (oo), with the symbol (ᴗ), for the short sound above it. 4. At the bottom write, *lettuce* and draw a picture, then on the right side, write (i), with the symbol (ᴗ), for the short sound above it.

Vowel (Uu)

Short (u)	Long (u) Vce/Silent (e)	Long (u) Open syllable when the first syllable is accented	Short (oo)	Short (i)
us	use	July	put	busy
up	rule	duty	pull	business
mum	tune	unit	full	busyness
fun	cube	unite	bull	minute
run	cute	jury	bullet	lettuce
pup	huge	ruby	push	
sum	June	stupid	bush	
nut	pure	music	pussy	
hug	refuse	cubic	butcher	
mud	excuse	student	pudding	

Can you think of words that fit the above patterns? Write them below.

Short (u)	Long (u) Vce/Silent (e)	Long (u) Open syllable when the first syllable is accented	Short (oo)	Short (i)

Consonant and Vowel, (Yy)

Tutors

A (y) says 1. Its name (y), as in _yes_. 2. Long vowel (e), as in _mummy_. 3. Long vowel (i), as in _my, reply_ and _cycle_. 4. Short vowel (i), as in _bicycle_. Choose words to illustrate, according to your artistic ability.

To make a flash card, write (y) in the middle of the card and capital (Y) at the bottom of the left-hand corner. On the back, divide the card into four sections. 1. On the top left-hand side write _yellow_, draw a picture underneath and on the right side, write (y). 2. Under this write _funny_, draw a picture and on the right side, write (e), with the symbol (-), for a long sound above it. 3. Under this write _sky_, draw a picture and on the right side, write (i), with the symbol (-), for a long sound above it. 4. Under this, write, _bicycle_, draw a picture and on the right side, write (i), with the symbol (ᴗ), for the short sound above it.

Consonant and Vowel (Yy)

Y consonant	Long (i) 1 or 2 syllable words make a long (i) sound.	Long (i) Open syllable or a VCe	Short (i) Closed syllable	Long (e) 2 or more syllable words make a long (e) sound.
yes	my	cycle	bicycle	mummy
you	by	style	gymnastics	daddy
your	cry	type	system	lady
yell	fly	typing	syllable	baby
yellow	dry	cycling	Olympic	funny
yet	sky	cyclone	pyjamas	tiny
yam	reply	cyber	crystal	only
yum	deny	stylish	symbol	many
yawn	rely	cycled	platypus	silly
young	July	types	cryptic	slowly

Can you think of words that fit the above patterns? Write them below.

Y consonant	Long (i) 1 or 2 syllable words make a long (i) sound.	Long (i) Open syllable or a VCe	Short (i) Closed syllable	Long (e) 2 or more syllable words make a long (e) sound.

Glossary

Auditory processing: Is when your brain perceives and uses a sound. It is *what we do with what we hear*. A person can have good hearing (their ears are sending the sound to their brain) but have poor *auditory processing* (their brain doesn't match up the sounds accurately). Processing what is heard can be slower in some people and this can affect learning.

Conceptual: Relating to ideas based on mental concepts that may have multiple of possible answers. It is concerned with the definitions or relationships of concepts of some field of enquiry, rather than with the facts.

Consonant: Are thought of as sounds that are only produced together with vowels to form a syllable. They are all the letters of the English alphabet that are not vowels: *b, c, d, f, g, h, j, k, l, m, n, p, q, r, s, t, v, w, x, y, z.*

Critical thinking: An objective analysis and evaluation of facts or an issue; to form a judgement or to evaluate, analyse and interpret the merits and faults of a piece of work.

Decoding: Is a word attack skill involving a process of translating a printed word into its sounds or phonemes, e.g. *jump* has four phonemes, e.g. *j-u-m-p.*

Digraphs: The combination of two letters that often represent one sound; e.g. *th*, in *them* and *ch* in *church*. The two letters forming a *digraph* are not to be separated when decoding.

Dyslexia: Can be referred to as a Specific Learning Disability. It is a developmental disorder which can cause a learning difficulty in the areas of reading, writing, and or numeracy. It can be referred to as word blindness, which is a reading disorder associated with the impairment of the ability to interpret spatial relationships or to integrate auditory and visual information.

Homophone: A word that is pronounced the same as another word, but has a different meaning and or spelling, e.g. meet and meat. You need to listen to the context of a sentence to know what the word means.

Homograph: Are words that have the same spelling, but differ in meaning and origin, whether pronounced the same way or not, e.g. *bear* [1]"to carry; support" and *bear* [2]"animal."

Inference: A conclusion reached from evidence and reasoning. It is the process of inferring; we guess or form an opinion based on the information that we know or have, which can be referred to as reading between the lines.

Literal: Follows the words of the original very closely and accurately; true to fact; not exaggerated; actual or factual.

Metacognition: Thinking about one's mental process of higher-order thinking that enables understanding, analysis, and control of one's cognitive processes, especially when engaged in learning.

Mnemonics: A technique of improving or developing the memory, such as to remember how to spell a word, e.g. using the first letter of words, *Enough Now Or Uncle Gets Hurt* spells *enough*.

Multisensory: Relates to involving or using more than one of the senses, e.g. seeing, speaking, hearing, feeling or doing.

Multisyllabic: A word that has many syllables, e.g. *mul-ti-syl-la-bic.*

Nonsense words: These are pseudowords or non-words that have no meaning. They are used to indicate if a reader can pronounce words into their phonemes or sounds, to read or write, e.g. *quafe, phiny.*

Phonemes: Are letters of a writing system in a language that have a distinctive unit of speech sound, that distinguishes one word from another, to indicate a difference in meaning, e.g. *b* from *p*, in *pit* and *bit.*

Phonemic Awareness: Is the ability to hear, identify and manipulate individual sounds or phonemes in spoken words, which includes manipulating units of oral languages, such as words, syllables, and onset and rimes. Students should be able to make and identify: oral rhymes, clap the number of syllables in words and recognise words that start or end with the same sound or have the same vowel sound. It is the foundation for spelling and words recognition skills.

Phonics: Is a method of teaching reading and spelling and how to pronounce words by learning the phonetic value of letters, letter groups, and especially syllables, to develop students' phonemic awareness so that they can determine and distinguish between phonemes to spell and read.

Prefix: Is added to the beginning of an existing word to change its meanings, e.g. add *un* to *happy* to make *unhappy.*

Schwa: A *schwa* is a lazy vowel sound. Often the unstressed vowel sound becomes a schwa, e.g. *the (thu), about (ubout) and freedom (freedim).*

Short-term memory (or "primary" or "active memory"): Is the capacity for holding a small amount of information in the mind in an active, readily available state for a short period. The duration of *short-term memory* is believed to be in the order of seconds. This impairment affects learning.

Suffix: Is added to the end of an existing word to change its meaning, e.g. add *less* to *taste* to make *tasteless.*

Syllables: Must have one or more vowel sound, with or without consonants, that form part or the whole part of a word. There are **closed, open syllables and irregular syllables**. They are divided according to how they are stressed. In closed syllables, e.g. *CVC/CVC,* as in *win/ter,* the vowel is a short sound when the first syllable is stressed and the consonant is at the end of the syllable. In open syllables, e.g. *CV/CVC,* as in *mu/sic,* the vowel is a long sound when the first syllable is stressed and the vowel is at the end of the syllable. In irregular syllables, e.g. *CVC/VC,* as in *riv/er,* the vowel is a short sound when the second syllable is stressed.

Trigraphs: The combination of three letters to represent one sound; e.g. *thr,* in *three* and *spl* in *splash.* The three letters forming a *trigraph* are not to be separated.

Visual processing: Is the ability to make sense of information taken in through the eyes which is different from problems involving sight or sharpness of vision. Difficulties with visual processing affect how visual information is interpreted or processed by the brain. Slower processing can affect the speed with which someone takes in information to learn.

Vowels: A letter representing a vowel, as in English, *a, e, i, o, u,* and sometimes *y.* Vowels can have short, long and schwa sounds, e.g. an (*a*) as in: *at, ate, all, any, was, shortage, about, visa.*

Core Sight Words

Core words should be learnt so that they are read and spelt automatically, without any sounding out. These are some of the most commonly spelt words to read and write.

arc	was	his	have
has	this	here	went
and	put	they	you
now	come	comes	one
after	again	some	your
how	what	said	for
all	does	from	who
any	many	could	would
should	want	before	each
which	other	use	these
about	their	goes	large
right	always	water	more
people	know	because	another
very	before	friend	beginning
down	long	were	part
new	find	better	once
young	school	children	almost
number	follow	sentence	answer
picture	often	first	word
around	between	enough	began
every	money	through	walk
together	thought	whose	won't
don't	what's	couldn't	should've

Consonants, Vowels, Digraphs and Trigraphs

Consonants

There are 21 consonants in the English language:

Consonant	As in:
b	**b**oat
c	1. **c**at. 2. Soft (s): (c) followed by (e), (i) and (y) can say (s), e.g. **ce**nt, **ci**ty and **cy**cle
d	**d**og
f	**f**rog
g	1. **g**ot 2. Soft (j): (g) followed by (e), (i) and (y) can say (j), e.g. **ge**ntle, **gi**raffe and **gy**m
h	**h**im
j	**j**ump
k	**k**itten
l	**l**ittle
m	**m**y
n	**n**ine
p	**p**up
q	1. (kw), **qu**ick, (q) is always followed by (u), e.g. (qu) 2. (k), mos**qu**ito
r	**r**un
s	1. (s), **s**un 2. (z), wa**s** and reali**s**e
v	**v**an
w	**w**ax
x	1. (ks), si**x** 2. (z), **x**ylophone, (x) says (z) at the beginning of a word
y	1. (y), **y**ellow 2. Long (e), bab**y** 3. Long (i), cr**y** and c**y**cle 4. Short (i), c**y**st
z	**z**oo

Vowels

There are 5 vowels: a, e, i, o, u and sometimes y. (See consonant (y), above)

Vowel	As in:
(Aa)	1. Short (a), **at** 2. Long (a), **late** and **lazy** 3. (ar), **father** 4. Short (o), **want** and **squad**, as (w) often says short (o), after a (w) sound 5. (or), **ball** 6. Short (e), **any** 7. Short (i), **cabbage** 8. Short (u), **about** and **Lisa**, (a) can say short (u), at the beginning and end of words
(Ee)	1. Short (e), **get** 2. Long (e), **here** and **begin** 3. Short (i), **seven**
(Ii)	1. Short (i), **him** 2. Long (i), **like** and **tiger** 3. Long (e), **kiwi** and **radio**
(Oo)	1. Short (o), **not** 2. Long (o), **home** and **open** 3. Long (oo), **to** 4. Short (u), **come**
(Uu)	1. Short (u), **mum** 2. Long (u), **cube** and **July** 3. Short (oo), **put** 4. Short (i), **busy** and **minute**

Digraphs and Trigraphs

Di/Trigraphs	As in:
sh	**sh**ip and di**sh**
th	1. (th), blowing, **th**ing and wi**th** 2. (th), tongue behind top teeth, **th**em 3. (t), **Th**omas and Es**th**er, often in names
wh	1. (w), **wh**en 2. (h), **wh**o, when (wh) is followed by an (o), the (w) is silent
ch	1. (ch), **ch**ur**ch** 2. (k), s**ch**ool, a silent (h) 3. (sh), ma**ch**ine
ng	si**ng**, sa**ng**, su**ng** and so**ng**, used after a short vowel sound
ck	(k), ba**ck**, used after a short vowel sound
gn	(n), silent (g), **gn**at and si**gn**

kn	(n), silent (k), **kn**ow
mb	(m), silent (b), la**mb**
bt	(t), silent (b), de**bt**
wr	(r), silent (w), **wr**ite
ph	(f), **ph**oto
gh	1. (g), **gh**astly, at the beginning of a word 2. (gh) is silent after a vowel: hi**gh**, wei**gh**t, thou**gh**, tau**gh**t and strai**gh**t
gu	(g), **gu**ess, **gu**ard, as the (u) is often silent after (g)
pn	(n), silent (p), **pn**eumonia
rh	(r), silent (h), **rh**inoceros
dge	(j), bri**dge**, used after a short vowel sound
ed	1. (ed) or (id), shout**ed** and add**ed.** Words ending with (t) and (d) 2. (t), jump**ed**, sniff**ed**, lik**ed**, wish**ed**, bath**ed**, watch**ed**. Words ending in blowing sounds: (p), (f), (k), (sh), (th), (ch), the (ed) says (t), but they need to be spelt (ed) 3. (d), lov**ed**
ay	Long (a), d**ay**, used at the end of a word
ai	Long (a), w**ai**t, never used at the end of a word
ey	1. Long (a), th**ey** 2. Long (e), mon**ey**
ei	1. Long (a), v**ei**n 2. Long (e), rec**ei**ve 3. Short (i), forf**ei**t
eigh	Long (a), **eigh**t, (gh) is silent after a vowel
ee	Long (e), f**ee**t, always says long (e)
ea	1. Long (e), **ea**t 2. Short (e), br**ea**d 3. Long (a), st**ea**k
ew	1. Long (u), n**ew**, a (W) controlled vowel 2. Long (oo), bl**ew** 3. Long (o), s**ew** and s**ew**n
eu	Long (u), **Eu**rope and pn**eu**monia
igh	Long (i), l**igh**t, (gh) is silent after a vowel
ie	1. Long (i), p**ie** 2. Long (e), f**ie**ld 3. Short (e), fr**ie**nd
er	1. (er), f**er**n, an (R) controlled vowel 2. Short (u), moth**er**, a schwa sound 3. (ar), cl**er**k and H**er**vey
ir	(er), f**ir**st, an (R) controlled vowel

ur/urr	1. (er), **nur**se, an (R) controlled vowel 2. (er), **purr**
wor	(wer), **wor**ks, an (R) and (W) controlled vowel
yr	(er), **myr**tle, an (R) controlled vowel
ear	1. (er), **ear**ly, an (R) controlled vowel 2. Long (ear), h**ear** 3. (ar), h**ear**t
oa	1. Long (o), b**oa**t 2. (or), br**oa**d
oe	1. Long (o), t**oe** 2. Long (oo), sh**oe** 3. Short (u), d**oe**s
oo	1. Long (oo), t**oo** 2. Short (oo), t**oo**k 3. (or), p**oo**r 4. Short (u), b**loo**d
oy	(oy), b**oy**
oi	(oy), s**oi**l
ow	1. Long (o), sl**ow** 2. (ou), n**ow**
ou	1. (ow), r**ou**nd 2. Long (oo), y**ou** 3. (or), c**ou**rt 4. Long (o), s**ou**l 5. Short (u), c**ou**ntry 6. Short (oo), c**ou**ld
ough	1. Long (o), th**ough**, (gh) is silent after a vowel 2. Long (oo), thr**ough** 3. (uf), en**ough** 4. (of), c**ough** 5. (or), th**ough**t 6. (ow), b**ough**
ous	(us), fam**ous**
ue	1. Long (u), ven**ue** 2. Long (oo), bl**ue** 3. (ue), is often silent after a (g), vag**ue**
ui	1. Long (oo), fr**ui**t 2. Short (i), b**ui**ld
or/ore	(or), **for**m, an (R) controlled vowel (or), bef**ore**
aw	(or), s**aw**, a (W) controlled vowel

au	1. (or), **au**thor
	2. Short (o), **Au**stralia
war	(wor), **war**m, a (W) and (R) controlled vowel
ar/uar	1. (ar), d**ar**k, an (R) controlled vowel
	2. (ar), g**uar**d, silent (u)
	3. (air), p**ar**ent
air	(air), h**air**, an (R) controlled vowel
aer	(air), **aer**oplane, an (R) controlled vowel
are	(air), c**are**, an (R) controlled vowel
eer	(ear), b**eer**, an (R) controlled vowel
ear	(ear), h**ear**, an (R) controlled vowel
si	1. (sh), (sion) says (shon), se**ssi**on
	2. (zh), (sion) says (zhon), vi**si**on
ci	1. (sh), (cial) says (shall), spe**ci**al
	2. (sh), (cious) says (shuss), deli**ci**ous
	3. (sh), (cian) says (shan), musi**ci**an
ti	1. (sh), (tion) says (shon), addi**ti**on
	2. (sh), (tial) says (shall), ini**ti**al
	3. (sh), (tious) says (shuss), infec**ti**ous

Cards can be made to learn the phoneme's sound for each of the consonants, digraphs and trigraphs, as per the vowels. These cards should often be revised, as repetition is an excellent way of learning, especially for students with learning difficulties.

Printed in the United States
By Bookmasters